REVELS STUDENT EDITIONS

GALATEA
John Lyly

MANCHESTER
1824
Manchester University Press

REVELS STUDENT EDITIONS

Based on the highly respected Revels Plays, which provide a wide range of scholarly critical editions of plays by Shakespeare's contemporaries, the Revels Student Editions offer readable and competitively priced introductions, text and commentary designed to distil the erudition and insights of the Revels Plays, while focusing on matters of clarity and interpretation. These editions are aimed at undergraduates, graduate teachers of Renaissance drama and all those who enjoy the vitality and humour of one of the world's greatest periods of drama.

GENERAL EDITOR David Bevington

REVELS STUDENT EDITIONS

GALATEA
John Lyly

edited by Leah Scragg

MANCHESTER
UNIVERSITY PRESS

Published by Manchester University Press
Altrincham Street, Manchester M1 7JA
www.manchesteruniversitypress.co.uk

British Library Cataloguing-in-Publication Data is available

ISBN 978 07190 8805 6 paperback

First published 2012

The publisher has no responsibility for the persistence or accuracy of URLs for any external or third-party internet websites referred to in this book, and does not guarantee that any content on such websites is, or will remain, accurate or appropriate.

Typeset by Topan Best-set Premedia Limited.

Contents

Introduction

Set in a world threatened with inundation, *Galatea* (or *Gallathea* as the title was spelled in the first printed edition)[1] might seem to be a parable for our time. Having violated the conditions that govern the universe in which they exist, the inhabitants of the play world are faced with a choice between making an intolerable sacrifice in order to preserve their way of life or falling victim to an elemental force, but are too wedded to self-interest, when the issue impinges on their own lives, to subjugate their needs to the welfare of the community as a whole. The description of the natural world upon which Tityrus, one of the drama's two father-figures, embarks at the outset of the play, when informing his daughter of the danger in which she stands, offers a curiously modern view of the world as undergoing successive periods of climatic change that transform the land's seemingly stable contours, destroying established life-forms, and enabling new ecosystems to arise. The vision that he offers to the audience of an endless time-span in the course of which the seas ebb and flow (1.1.15ff.) is wholly at odds with the Biblical view of the universe that would have been current when the play was composed, with form, and God's immutable order, imposed upon chaos at the moment of creation, but it speaks directly to the modern consciousness, attuned to Darwinian theory and aware, from a childhood preoccupation with prehistoric life-forms, of the waves of extinction that reach back through geological time.

It is not merely the dangerous fluidity of the natural world presented in the play that strikes a chord, moreover, with the twenty-first-century reader or spectator. Unlike the majority of early modern dramatic works, the play has a preponderance of female roles, and the construction of gender, like the physical environment of the play, is markedly at odds with the notion of an unchanging, divinely ordained natural order or condition. The two central figures, Galatea and Phillida, disguised as boys by their fathers at the outset, fall in love with one another at their first exchange, and conduct a coded courtship throughout the action that calls in question the foundations of sexual attraction as understood by those to whom the work

1

was originally addressed. At the same time, as girls to themselves and their fathers, but youths to one another and Diana's nymphs, Galatea/ Tityrus and Phillida/Melibeus occupy an ambivalent position in gender terms, and their experience implicitly interrogates the construction of socio-sexual relationships in force when the drama was composed. Ambiguous in the eyes of the audience from her first entrance, in that she is addressed by her companion as a woman while being dressed in masculine attire, Galatea sees her translation into a male persona not in terms of a shift from the emotional to the rational, or the assumption of a higher place in the order of being, but of an adjustment to fresh occupations, and a transfer from the domestic to the public sphere (cf. 'I will now use for the distaff the bow, and play at quoits abroad that was wont to sew in my sampler at home': 2.4.10–12), while her determination to model her conduct on that of another youth (cf. 'But whist, here cometh a lad. I will learn of him how to behave myself': 2.1.12–13)[2] implies that gender roles are socially determined, and performed rather than innate. The fact that a change of clothes is sufficient to make the disguised maidens desirable not only to one another but to the followers of Diana further destabilizes the demarcation of gender boundaries, while the triggering of love by Cupid's arrows (signifying amatory desire) implies the contingency of sexual attraction.

Nevertheless, for all the seeming modernity that has made *Galatea* the most frequently acted of Lyly's plays in recent times (see pp. 24ff. below), the radical instability that informs the dramatist's construction of both the human and the natural worlds is rooted in a set of circumstances unique to the period in which the drama was produced. The stylized nature of its dramatic language, the sources upon which it draws, the genre to which it belongs, the audience to which it was directed, and the company by which it was performed all bear witness to a work deeply embedded in the late sixteenth-century cultural landscape, offering the twenty-first-century spectator a window upon a kind of theatrical event wholly at odds with the work and working environment of more familiar early modern writers, such as Marlowe and Shakespeare. The first significant dramatist of the early modern period, Lyly wrote for the court and the private theatres rather than for the public stage (see pp. 4 and 14ff. below), precipitated into the role of purveyor of dramatic entertainments for the intellectual elite through the vogue created by the prose style that he inaugurated in his first published work, and which remained the cornerstone of his subsequent success. It is consequently with the 'new English'[3] upon which his career was founded, rather than the more obviously approachable aspects of his plays, that it is arguably most useful to begin an exploration of the simultaneous immediacy and distance of *Galatea*.

LANGUAGE AND STRUCTURE: FROM A PROSE STYLE TO A DRAMATIC MODE

Born into a family deeply involved in the humanist movement, John Lyly (1554?–1606) clearly regarded himself as destined not for a career in the newly burgeoning entertainment industry but for academic advancement. The eldest son of an official at Canterbury cathedral, and a grandson of William Lily, High Master of St Paul's School and author of the Latin grammar that was to form the bedrock of the teaching of Latin in England for over three hundred years, he was probably educated at the King's School in Canterbury,[4] before going up to Magdalen College, Oxford, where his grandfather and uncle had studied before him. His university experience did not live up, however, to his expectations,[5] and having been denied a university fellowship he was obliged to leave Oxford, and to make a living by other means. His first foray into the literary sphere, *Euphues: The Anatomy of Wit*, a prose work published in 1578, was an instant success, encouraging him to produce an expanded edition the following year, and then a sequel, *Euphues and His England*, in 1580. Numerous editions followed in the course of the next forty years, firmly establishing the work as the most popular, and widely imitated, secular composition of the age.[6] The literary sensation created by the two parts of the work was largely a product not of their subject matter but their style, and it was this style, seen by its admirers as imposing a new order on the structural exuberance of sixteenth-century English prose, and credited by Lyly's first editor with influencing the spoken language of the court,[7] which was to remain fundamental to Lyly's compositional habits throughout his working life.

At the heart of what is now known as the euphuistic mode is the use of antithesis as a vehicle for the exploration of complex ideas. Sentences characteristically evolve through contrasting clauses, with the oppositions between them emphasized through sound patterning, particularly assonance and alliteration. The aged Eubulus remarks, for example, to the youthful Euphues, 'Thou art here in Naples a young sojourner, I an old senior; thou a stranger, I a citizen; thou

secure doubting no mishap, I sorrowful dreading thy misfortune'
(pp. 36–7). Though the style clearly has its origins in academic
debate, implying the precise articulation of an argument, leading to
the exhibition of the superiority of one particular position, the insistent location in Lyly's work of an expanding series of alternative
potentialities branching outwards from an initial proposition serves
to undermine any sense of a drive towards closure, eroding rather
than promoting certainty, and precluding finality through the implication that every contention is capable of revision, and may be
countered or reversed. The pervasive ambivalence generated by the
mode is furthered, moreover, by word-play (e.g. the use of homophones and puns) demonstrating the capability of terms to carry
contrary meanings, and by the extensive use of imagery, largely
drawn from proverbial wisdom, exotic natural history, or classical
myth, exhibiting the contrasting properties of natural phenomena
and thus their capacity for change to an opposite state.[8] Together,
the features of the style promote the perception of a pervasive
duality informing every aspect of both the human and natural
worlds, and a universal potential for mutation into an antithetical
physical or mental condition.

   Though there is no evidence that Lyly had any aspirations to write
for the theatre prior to the composition of the works that marked
his entrance onto the literary scene, the success of the two parts of
Euphues led to his installation by the Earl of Oxford (then seeking
to reinstate himself in the favour of the Queen) at the first Blackfriars theatre (see pp. 14ff. below), with a view to the composition of
plays for performance at court. His first two plays, *Campaspe* and
Sappho and Phao, structured on the antithetical patterning now
synonymous with his work, inaugurated a wholly original comic
form, and by the time of his third play, *Galatea*, composed circa
1584, euphuism had evolved in Lyly's hands from a mechanism for
the organization of complex ideas into the structural basis of a highly
sophisticated dramatic mode.

   The see-saw oppositions characteristic of the prose style now
radiate into every aspect of the composition, from the dramatic
language (see Cupid's account of love at 1.2.18–19 as 'A heat full of
coldness, a sweet full of bitterness, a pain full of pleasantness' and
Telusa's reflections on her predicament at the start of 3.1), through
the relationships and exchanges between the dramatis personae (e.g.
Galatea and Tityrus in 1.1, Cupid and a nymph of Diana in 1.2,
Venus and Diana in 5.3), to visual contrasts of gender or age (e.g.
Galatea and Tityrus in 1.1, Cupid and Diana in 3.4). Scenes function

as mirror images of one another (e.g. the girl/boy disguise already in place in 1.1, reversed in the boy/girl disguise proposed at the close of 1.2, and projected in the girl/boy disguise discussed by Melebeus and Phillida in 1.3), while the sub-plot involving the adventures of Robin, Rafe, and Dick reverses the terms of the main plot in being centred upon male rather than female experience, and authority figures who claim a divine state rather than disguise one (see p. 8 below). Characters and stage properties embody the 'doubleness'[9] insistently enforced through the punning and imagery of euphuistic prose (e.g. the sexual ambivalence of the central couple and the tree that offers Galatea and Tityrus protection from the sun while being the site of the virgin sacrifice that threatens the former's life).

The awareness of mutability invading every aspect of experience promoted by the two prose works is similarly projected in dramatic terms – in, for example, the exchanges and pretensions of the characters (e.g. Tityrus' opening account of the changing landscape, and the Alchemist's claim to transform base metals into gold), reversals of attitude (e.g. the chaste nymphs of Diana becoming consumed by sexual desire), shifts of authority (e.g. Cupid's transformation from a 'great god' (1.2.34) to 'Diana's slave' (3.4.105)), the use of disguise (cf. Cupid's assumption of female attire), and physical change (cf. the projected metamorphosis of either Phillida or Galatea at the close of the play). Even the stage properties bear witness to the instability of the play world. The 'heap of small pebble' (1.1.15) on stage at the outset of the play was once, Tityrus informs us, 'a stately temple of white marble' (1.1.16), while the spar on which the boys are tossed ashore in 1.4 was formerly a part of the Mariner's ship.

As in the two prose works, insistent word-play also contributes to the representation of an unstable world, capable of translation into new and unfamiliar forms. Everyday terms prove to carry different meanings for different speakers (e.g. 'card' and 'point' in 1.4, 'spirit' in 2.3), while specialized language frustrates rather than promotes communication (cf. the hunting terms of 2.1, the alchemical vocabulary of 2.3, and the astronomical jargon of 3.3), implying that the characters inhabit discrete linguistic (and hence mental) worlds. Homophones (e.g. deer/dear in 2.1), puns (e.g. would/wood in 2.3), and the dislocation of terms from their semantic roots (e.g. 'Concur? Condog!' at 3.3.28) contribute to the creation of a lexis that defies the articulation of unequivocal meaning, heightening the 'doubleness' of the play world, while the duality pervading the action is projected beyond the scope of the drama itself through the quibbling responses by which the boys agree to sing at the marriage orchestrated by Venus in the final scene.

In the light of the process of change at work in every aspect of the play, the physical transformation that resolves the unfulfillable love of the central couple emerges not as a dramatic device designed to impose an arbitrary solution on an intractable situation but as a further exhibition of the fluidity of a universe in which mutation is a primary condition. The euphuistic mode, and the highly patterned antithetical structuring that derives from it, is thus an inseparable adjunct of the plot, enacting the shifts and reversals of an unstable world. Nevertheless, for all the centrality of the mode to the definition of the universe projected by the work, the metamorphoses that take place in the course of the drama have their literary origins elsewhere, and it is to the sources on which Lyly drew in constructing his play that it is necessary to turn next for an understanding of the embeddedness of the work in the cultural forms of its own age.

OVID AND VIRGIL

Though only one of the eight plays by Lyly that have survived to modern times is directly structured on a particular source,[10] all of his comedies exhibit the classical learning common to the sixteenth-century educated elite, and make frequent use of Latin quotations designed to flatter the audience to which his works were directed through the implication of a shared, superior understanding. A large number of classical authors are utilized in the course of the plays, either by allusion or direct quotation, but by far the most frequently cited is Ovid (43 BC–AD 18), an author whose works, widely used as an educational instrument in Tudor classrooms, had a major influence on a number of notable sixteenth-century writers, including Shakespeare. Three myths that Ovid relates in his *Metamorphoses* are woven together in *Galatea*: the story of Iphis, a maiden who, having been disguised as a boy at birth by her mother to escape the death ordained by her father should she prove to be a girl, falls in love with another maiden, Ianthe, and is transformed into a youth by Isis to enable their love to be fulfilled (*Metamorphoses*, bk ix, lines 666–797);[11] the tale of Hesione, a daughter of Laomedon, King of Troy, who is bound to a rock as an offering to a sea-monster, sent by an enraged Poseidon (Greek equivalent of Neptune) to ravage the land, when the Trojans renege on a payment due to him for his help (*Metamorphoses*, bk xi, lines 199–215); and the history of Galatea, a sea-nymph beloved of Acis, but pursued by the Cyclops, Polyphemus (*Metamorphoses*, bk xiii, lines 730–897). All three tales turn on some species of metamorphosis, in accordance with the theme of the Ovidian poem as a whole, exhibiting, in the words of the work's most celebrated sixteenth-century translator, 'That nothing under heaven doth ay in steadfast state remain', and that 'each substance takes / Another shape than that it had'.[12] Thus, having fallen in love with another woman, Isis is changed at her marriage into a youth (cf. the outcome of the mistaken affections of the Lylian play); the angry Neptune transforms the Trojan landscape when denied the sum to which he is due (cf. Tityrus' account of the consequences of arousing Neptune's wrath at *Galatea*, 1.1.15ff.);[13] while the Ovidian Galatea causes her lover to become a river when the furious Cyclops intends his death (cf. the name that Lyly assigns to his central figure and the unstable riverine setting of the work).

Though the dramatist clearly embraces the notion of change at the heart of his classical model, however, his treatment of the stories on which he draws is far more evasive than their handling in the classical source. While Ovid's tales are designed to illustrate an inexorable process of change, and are largely uncomplicated in terms of the sympathies that they evoke (e.g. for the maternal affection prompting the disguise of Isis, and the gross ingratitude that causes Neptune to take his revenge), the situations that Lyly creates are much more problematic, arousing divided responses among those both inside and outside the play world, and shifts of attitude on the part of the audience as the action evolves. The virgin sacrifice that lies at the heart of the action and prompts the disguise of the two central figures may be seen, for example, as both a legitimate recompense for a gross act of impiety (the stance adopted by Neptune), and a hideous act of violation (suggested through his instrument, the Agar). Similarly, Tityrus' decision to conceal his daughter may be regarded as the product of commendable paternal love, but it is also an attempt to evade the wishes of a deity (running in direct opposition, in the minds of a sixteenth-century audience, to Abraham's willingness to sacrifice his son: Genesis 22, 1–18), and a refusal to set the public good before private affections. Though the two father-figures appear commendable, if misguided, in the opening scenes in their attempts to save their daughters from a terrible death, by the close they emerge as essentially selfish, powerless in the face

of forces far larger than themselves, and motivated by trivial concerns (see their dispute in 5.3 over whose daughter should be transformed into a youth).

The material that Lyly grafts on to his Ovidian tales similarly
invites construction in a variety of ways. Cupid's disguise as a girl,
which functions as a mirror-image of the disguises adopted by Phillida and Galatea, is motivated by a desire for revenge that parallels
Neptune's in being warranted by a sleight, but it too appears cruel
in the suffering it occasions, arousing sympathy for the targets of his
malice, and a revision of attitudes in relation to the concepts they
embody (see pp. 12ff. below). When Cupid himself is captured by
Diana, however, the stance of the audience is reversed, with the
upholders of chastity appearing cruel in their revenge, deriding him
as powerless and subjecting him to physical assault (cf. his clipped
wings and the violence threatened by the Agar). The sub-plot activities of Robin, Rafe, and Dick also serve to complicate the way in
which the concerns of the main plot are viewed. The three boys
encounter a succession of masters, each concerned in some way with
the usurpation of divine power and claiming the capacity to transform (cf. the transformations threatened by Neptune and effected
by Cupid and Venus). The Mariner holds the sea in contempt ('I
fear the sea no more than a dish of water': 1.4.39–40), and ambigu-
ously claims the ability to 'shift the moon and the sun' (1.4.35); the
Alchemist asserts the power to change base metals into gold; the
Astrologer declares his ability to foretell the future, metamorphose
thoughts (3.3.85), and place Rafe's intellectual capacities on a par
with the gods' (3.3.80–1); while the cozener encountered by Dick
seeks to reverse the order of nature by a reordering of the boys'
family tree (5.1.71ff.). While all four men are patently ludicrous in
their claims, the terms in which the first three voice their aspirations
offer a view of divinity far grander than that projected by the
offended and quarrelling deities who stand at the centre of the
action of the play (see the claims of the Alchemist at 2.3.133ff.),
undermining the stature of divine beings willing to shroud their
godhead for petty ends (cf. Neptune's disguise as a shepherd proposed in 2.2).

The shifts of perspective engineered by the dramatist through his
evasive handling of his Ovidian source, together with the pervasive
ambiguity generated by the style, give rise to a species of composition that, to use G. K. Hunter's analogy, may be likened to a piece
of shot silk,[14] in that it is capable of yielding different meanings

according to the perspective from which it is viewed – and the 'doubleness' informing every aspect of the work is further promoted by the dramatist's deployment of a second classical source, pointedly evoked at the outset of the play. The names of the two father-figures of the drama are drawn from *Eclogues* of the Roman poet Virgil, another familiar sixteenth-century classroom text, and the opening suggestion by Tityrus that he and his daughter should seek the shade of a tree to avoid the heat of the sun echo the opening lines of the classical work.

Virgil's *Eclogues* consists of a sequence of poems firmly located in the pastoral tradition, a highly non-naturalistic literary genre that has its origins in ancient Greece, and which deploys rustic figures, principally goatherds and shepherds, in an idealized Arcadian landscape, governed by classical deities but far removed from the actualities of any specific place or time, as a vehicle for the exploration of highly refined emotional states, and for the discussion, in the hands of some writers, of political issues. The term 'shepherd', in the context of the pastoral tradition, is thus synonymous with 'lover', and the piping of music with the composition of poetic effusions, while the convention itself constitutes a means of 'speaking otherwise', or seeming to talk of one thing while referring to another. As used by Virgil, the mode permitted reference not only to amatory affairs but to the effects of a contemporary civil war,[15] though the speakers throughout are rustic figures, nominally engaged in tending their flocks.

The allusions to Virgil's work at the outset of *Galatea* invite the location of the play within the pastoral convention, and the drama conforms to the inherited genre in a range of respects. Though the action is ostensibly set on the banks of the river Humber, and the world that the characters inhabit is subject, like the Lincolnshire of the play's initial spectators, to floods, the unbearable heat of the sun to which Tityrus refers in the opening scene suggests a Mediterranean rather than an English location, and the presence of classical deities among the dramatis personae contributes to the divorce of the play's setting from the England of real life. Similarly, though the action nominally takes place at some period subsequent to the Viking invasions of Anglo-Saxon England, the gods who govern the action are derived from ancient Rome, while the boys who wander in search of a master, like the charlatans they meet, are sixteenth-century figures, immediately recognizable to a contemporary spectator. The dramatis personae also conform to the figures that conventionally people the pastoral world, and their concerns accord with the mode's dominant motifs. The fathers of the lovers at the centre of the action are shepherds, the interest turns on amatory affairs, while the song that the boys are enlisted to sing beyond the scope of the drama is directly concerned with marital love.

As in Virgil's first eclogue, moreover, the situations of the play's lovers, particularly the conflicting impulses of Diana's nymphs, have resonances beyond the play world itself, and the tensions that they experience, like those articulated in the Virgilian work, would have carried highly sensitive political implications for those to whom the work was initially addressed. As noted above, Lyly's comedies were primarily designed for performance at court (see p. 4), and the play's relevance to its intended audience roots the work yet more deeply in a cultural environment entirely foreign to the twenty-first-century reader or spectator. It is thus to the nature of the entertainments provided for the monarch at the Elizabethan court that it is requisite to turn next for an understanding of the paradoxical topicality and timelessness of the play.

THE PASTORAL CONVENTION AND THE CULT OF THE VIRGIN QUEEN

Entertainments for the monarch in the late Tudor period were supplied in a number of locations. During the winter season, when the court was in residence in the capital, plays were performed in the banqueting halls of the royal palaces in and around London, notably Greenwich, where *Galatea* itself was played, according to the title-page of the first edition.[16] During the summer, by contrast, when the monarch (i.e. Elizabeth I) undertook a progress to the estates of the principal members of her court, entertainments frequently took place in the open air, in settings specifically designed for the mounting of extravagant shows of a variety of kinds. In both types of location the Queen herself constituted the focal point of the event, and her presence was frequently evoked as both spectator and participant in the action. The rural settings of the entertainments mounted in the course of her summer progress lent themselves to allegorical playlets exploiting the pastoral convention, in which the sovereign could be celebrated either as the deity resolving tensions or as the object of the devoted love of rustic figures, signifying her courtiers, for a being beyond their sphere. In an entertainment at

Sudely, for example, the Queen was addressed on her arrival by 'an old shepherd' offering both symbolic gifts and 'shepherds' religion' (i.e. the duty of her subjects), while she was called upon to afford her protection the following Sunday to the mythical Daphne, pursued by the infatuated Apollo.[17] Similar masques, plays, and pageants were mounted at court. In Peele's *The Arraignment of Paris*, for example, the mythical golden apple is awarded initially to Venus by Paris, as in the traditional story, but then transferred to 'Zabeta' (i.e. Elizabeth) by Diana, while the lost play *Phyllida and Corin*, performed at court in 1584, was patently a pastoral piece, turning on the subject of courtly love.[18]

Though the Queen was honoured and invoked in such works in a number of guises, it was as a classical goddess that she was most frequently represented, figuring as both an authority figure and an object of worship. Her wisdom invited an equation with Minerva or her Greek equivalent, Pallas Athena, while her exalted position and unmarried status allowed her representation as Diana, Cynthia, Artemis, etc. The displacement of Roman Catholicism and the cult of the Virgin Mary from the centre of English national life effected by the Reformation had situated the monarch at the head of both church and state, permitting an easy transfer of adulation from one virgin figure to another on the ascent of an unmarried queen to the throne, and enabling her to occupy a quasi-divine status in state propaganda and the literary effusions of the age. While contributing to her elevation in the public mind, however, the virgin condition of the monarch was simultaneously a matter of concern, in that it clearly represented a barrier to the perpetuation of the royal line, opening the door to competition between rival claimants for the throne, and threatening the security of the state. It is this tension between an idealized condition and the requirements of realpolitik that the pastoral convention, with its Arcadian setting and distance from the realities of everyday life, permitted sixteenth-century writers to explore, affording them a means, in an age when censorship precluded the overt discussion of matters of state, of ingratiating themselves with the monarch while offering a coded comment on the difficulties attendant upon her role.

The majority of Lyly's plays turn on matters of direct relevance to the sovereign before whom all but one of his comedies were probably performed.[19] His first play, *Campaspe*, for example, explores the capabilities and limitations of monarchical power through a fiction safely distanced from its Elizabethan context by being set in the classical past, while *Midas*, the sixth of his comedies to survive to modern times, compares the condition of a realm governed by a wise monarch (i.e. Elizabeth) with one governed by an ill-advised one (i.e. Philip of Spain), capitalizing on the national feeling generated by the defeat of the Spanish Armada. Lying between these two works are four plays which rely, to a greater or lesser extent, on the pastoral convention, and all four turn upon some species of tension between chastity and amatory desire, charting the increasing anxiety surrounding the Queen's unmarried condition, and exploring her relationship with the members of her court. In the first of the group, *Sappho and Phao* (1584), Cupid causes a monarch to fall in love with a man significantly below her in rank, only to transfer his own devotion to her when she masters her feelings in a symbolic enactment of her superiority to amatory desire. The play is unusual in its vivid representation of the personal struggle that the Queen undergoes, but its conclusion is conventional, in terms of court panegyric, in its celebration of the transcendent virtue of a monarch who is mistress of, rather than subject to, love.[20] It is to this work that Lyly pointedly refers in *Galatea* (see 5.3.93–4), the second play in the group, but the outcome of the conflict between love and chastity in the later comedy is far more ambiguous than in the earlier work.

For the Elizabethan spectator, attuned to the conventions of the age, it would have been clear from the outset of *Galatea* that the figure of Diana, goddess of chastity, was intended to reflect Elizabeth in her persona as the Virgin Queen. Her contempt for love, her insistence upon the spotless virtue of her attendants, and the dignity of her stance in contrast to the ungoverned conduct of those around her all accord with the conventional representation of a sovereign superior to fleshly desires. Significantly, however, it is Neptune, rather than Diana, who is the supreme deity of the play, and his stance towards the quarrelling goddesses who enact the tension between chastity and amatory desire is far more ambivalent than might be expected, given the context in which the work was performed. Called upon to arbitrate between Venus (whose son Diana holds captive), and Diana (whose nymphs have been stricken by Cupid with love), he is obliged to admit that, while he honours the latter, he loves the former, and the judgement he passes constitutes a compromise rather than a victory for either party. The remission of the virgin sacrifice, viewed as a triumph by Diana, is bought with the liberation of Cupid, and his response to his mother's regret at his changed appearance suggests that his power (derived from

Venus) is enhanced rather than diminished by the captivity he has endured (see 5.3.102–6). At the same time, the parting shots between the opposing deities invite the suggestion that the chaste mind, in common with every aspect of the play world, is subject to the process of change. While Diana repudiates Venus' contention that she 'cannot forbid him [Cupid] to wound' with the assertion that 'chastity is not within the level of his bow', Venus retorts that 'beauty is a fair mark to hit', implying that attractive women will always be subject to love (see 5.3.87–89).

The experience of the human characters at the centre of the drama offers a similarly complex view of the relationship between the opposing impulses that the competing deities embody. While Venus and Diana regard the conditions they represent as mutually exclusive, Galatea and Phillida explore more ambivalent emotional states, gripped by love for an object of uncertain gender, and loving with little hope of sexual fulfilment. Though Diana is initially dismissive when their misplaced affection for a person who proves to be of the same sex is disclosed ('things falling out as they do, you must leave these fond, fond affections': 5.3.132–3), Venus queries not the object but the nature of their passion, in an exchange that proposes a different understanding of chastity from that propounded by Diana throughout:

> *Venus.* Is your loves unspotted, begun with truth, continued with constancy, and not to be altered till death?
>
> (5.3.146–7)

The questions effect a divorce between chastity and virginity, enabling the coexistence of the former with marital love, implicitly offering a solution, on one level of the action, to the problem of providing a successor to the realm while upholding the transcendent virtue of the occupant of the throne.

The Epilogue tips the balance of the debate between love and chastity yet further in the favour of love. Whereas at the close of *Sappho and Phao* Sappho declares love to be 'a toy made for ladies' (5.2.104–5) that she herself will henceforward direct, the closing lines of *Galatea* are delivered by a lover, and exhort the members of the audience to 'yield' to their amatory instincts, and to 'Confess him [Love] a conqueror, whom ye ought to regard, sith it is unpossible to resist' (lines 10–11). The mutability that invades every aspect of the play world is reiterated, moreover, in terms that invite application to the virgin condition, with the assertion that 'Venus can make constancy fickleness, courage cowardice, modesty lightness ... tempering hardest hearts like softest wool' (lines 2–5). Though in Lyly's next work, *Endymion*, the dramatic universe is once again ruled by an unattainable virgin figure, in the fourth play of the group, *Love's Metamorphosis*, it is Cupid who is the supreme deity of the play world, and those who resist his injunctions are obliged, rather than persuaded, to love.

While dealing with human emotions that transcend the concerns of any specific time, *Galatea* is thus born of a cluster of anxieties and performance conditions peculiar to the period in which it was composed. Not only is the Prologue specifically directed towards the monarch, locating the play among a group of entertainments designed for a specific court, but the Queen herself is the focus of the action, in that it is her predicament that lies at the heart of the work and to her that it ultimately speaks. The drama is overtly submitted to her judgement (cf. Prologue, lines 8–11), and implicitly located in her mind (cf. Prologue, lines 13–18), and it was consequently only when performed in her presence, before a courtly audience attentive to her response, that its realization as an artistic construct was complete. At the same time, however, the pastoral convention, with its classical origins, non-naturalistic setting, and indirectness of expression positions the work in an arena entirely distinct from the day-to-day realities of the environment in which it was initially performed, affording it a pertinence beyond the cultural context from which it emerged. Its diplomatic distance from the world that it critiques was furthered, moreover, by another aspect of sixteenth-century practice remote from the conventions of the twenty-first-century stage – the nature of the company by which it was performed.

LYLIAN DRAMA AND THE BOYS OF ST PAUL'S

Unlike the more familiar plays of the early modern period (e.g. the works of Marlowe and Shakespeare), *Galatea* was written not for a company of adult actors but for a juvenile troupe. Whereas, in the twenty-first century, performances of plays by groups of boys are amateur and occasional events, usually associated with end-of-term school activities, and often embarrassing in execution for all but the proudest of doting spectators, in the sixteenth century they constituted a staple of aristocratic entertainment, offering a more sophisticated type of histrionic diversion than that supplied by the travelling players, or the adult actors at the newly emergent public theatres.

The origins of the boy players, who were eventually to offer a threat to even the most successful of the adult troupes, including Shakespeare's company at the Globe,[21] lay in the use of acting as an educational instrument in the humanist grammar schools of the early sixteenth century as a means of promoting confidence and inculcating the art of public speaking. The poise and verbal facility acquired by the boys in the course of their training led to their enlistment by the owners of the great houses in the vicinity of their schools for the provision of seasonal recreation (e.g. at Christmas), or for the entertainment of guests, while the choir boys in attendance upon the monarch were required to fulfil a similar function in relation to the head of state, becoming a species of household players (the Children of the Chapel), tasked with the amusement of the sovereign, and the enhancement, through their accomplishments, of the ruler's prestige.

The development of such juvenile troupes into companies whose recreational function took precedence over their academic training and ecclesiastical role took a further step forward in 1576, when Richard Farrant leased a set of rooms in the Blackfriars for the rehearsal of plays designed for performance before the Queen by the Children of the Chapel, and admitted the paying public to watch. The concept of the performances being merely rehearsals was quickly abandoned in the light of the venture's success, and the First Blackfriars Theatre came into being – a venue markedly at odds with the large, open-air, 'public' playhouse opened by James Burbage in the same year, which afforded the model for the majority of the theatres eventually occupied by the adult troupes, and would ultimately supply the framework of the Globe.

Since the rooms leased by Farrant were designed to replicate the environment in which entertainments before the monarch took place, the playing space was a small one, allowing a far more intimate actor–audience relationship than was possible on the public stage, while the room was roofed and artificially lit, enabling a range of special effects. The performers were boys, ranging in age from eight to fifteen or sixteen, though it is possible that their masters may occasionally have undertaken some adult roles, when a substantial physique was required. The small size of the auditorium necessitated the charging of higher prices than at the much larger public theatres, leading in turn to a more affluent and highly educated clientele, approximating to the type of spectator for whom the plays were ultimately designed. It was at this 'private' playhouse that

Lyly was installed as resident dramatist by the Earl of Oxford following the success of his first published work (see p. 4 above), and here that his first two plays, *Campaspe* and *Sappho and Phao*, were initially performed by a combined troupe drawn from the Children of the Chapel and the Boys of St Paul's. The fact that *Galatea* was registered in the Stationers' Register in 1585 (see p. 22 below) suggests that it was written for the same venue, though no production of the play is recorded until 1588, when it was performed before the Queen at Greenwich by the Boys of St Paul's, a company with which Lyly was associated throughout his career following the closure of the First Blackfriars in 1584.

The comedies composed by Lyly for the juvenile troupes are notable for the skill with which the dramatist marries the requirements of the plays to the theatrical environment in which they were staged and the capabilities of his boy performers. Casts are invariably large, minimizing the strain on any particular member of the troupe, while the majority of the dramatis personae are women, young lovers, and boys, exploiting the slightness of build of the young performers, the epicene nature of their appearance, and the proximity, in the case of the last, between themselves and their roles.[22] Their capacity for rote learning is utilized in long speeches, designed for polished delivery rather than the enactment of emotional states, while their classical training is exhibited in the frequent use of Latin quotations, word games, and references to familiar classroom texts (cf. the allusion to Virgil's *Eclogues* at *Galatea*, 1.1.1–5), enlisting audience involvement through the implied appeal to a sophisticated understanding. Songs (e.g. at *Galatea*, 1.4.87ff.), and dancing with instrumental accompaniment (see *Galatea*, 2.3.6.1), capitalize on both the musical training of the choir schools to which the boys primarily belonged and the acoustic capabilities of a limited space, while echoing quasi-choric exchanges (e.g. *Galatea*, 3.1.98ff.) draw on the boys' experience in performing together as a troupe.

It is not merely the singing, dancing, and 'playing' (see *Galatea*, 2.3.6.1), moreover, which align the plays with the musical compositions that the boys were accustomed to perform. Scenes echo one another (cf. *Galatea*, 1.1. and 1.3), speakers catch up one another's words and phrases, while the use of 'serial' entrances (i.e. the appearance of a succession of characters enunciating similar positions) has analogies with the procedures of part-singing or dance (cf. the successive entrances of *Galatea*, 3.1). Lyly himself compares the first of the plays in the group to which *Galatea* belongs (see pp. 12ff. above) to a 'dance of a fairy in a circle' (*Sappho and Phao*, Epilogue, line 10),[23] and the analogy is literalized (among other places) at *Galatea* 2.3.6.1.

The diminutive size and plangent voices of the boy actors by whom the plays were performed, together with the quasi-musical structuring of the actions, the non-naturalistic nature of the settings, and the pastoral or classical worlds in which the events of the comedies take place, create a type of exquisite, otherworldly drama, seemingly remote in its self-conscious artifice from the politically charged realities of the environment for which the plays were ultimately designed. The elusiveness that invades every aspect of *Galatea*, thus extends to the production itself, which at once celebrates the monarch and addresses her concerns while operating in a realm entirely removed, in every respect, from the actualities of the day-to-day world. At the same time, deeply embedded in a type of cultural activity for which no twenty-first-century counterpart exists, the play allows the modern reader an insight into a type of courtly entertainment wholly unlike that supplied by the adult actors of the Elizabethan–Jacobean public stage, while simultaneously floating free, through its non-naturalism, of the historical circumstances from which it emerged, and thus inviting reinterpretation. It was an invitation that later writers and directors were quick to embrace.

LYLY AND SHAKESPEARE

Though relatively few people today are familiar with Lyly's work, in late sixteenth-century England it constituted a highly significant feature of the nation's cultural life. Not only were his two prose works the most frequently reprinted secular compositions of the age, but his first comedy, *Campaspe*, ran through four editions in under ten years, and all his plays had appeared in print, including *Galatea*, published in 1592, before his death in 1606. Celebrated by Lodge for his 'facility in discourse',[24] ranked by Francis Meres as among 'the best for comedy amongst us',[25] and singled out for mention by Ben Jonson in his encomium on Shakespeare prefacing the First Folio (1623), his work was imitated, applauded, plundered, and reviled, demonstrably known, in short, by his fellow writers and a wide spectrum of the reading public at large.

Of the many literary figures of the age who drew on Lyly's work, the dramatist who was eventually to eclipse the entire generation of writers who inaugurated the flowering of the Elizabethan–Jacobean stage is by far the most interesting to us today. Innumerable references throughout the Shakespearian corpus bear witness to the dramatist's close engagement with the Lylian canon as a whole, but it was *Galatea* that appears to have exercised the greatest hold on his imagination and to which he returned most frequently in the course of his career. Three plays in particular – *Love's Labour's Lost, As You Like It*, and *Twelfth Night* – bear the stamp of Lyly's work, but the use that Shakespeare makes of his predecessor's material differs markedly from play to play.[26]

The love of word-play characteristic of the Lylian corpus finds an obvious echo in the feast of arcane languages and exuberant word games of *Love's Labour's Lost*. Like *Galatea*, the play explores the tension between celibacy and sexual love, and it is the dance-like structure of the Lylian drama (intimately related to its highly patterned language) through which that theme is explored which clearly impressed the later writer and which he replicates in his own work. As in *Galatea*, the action evolves through a series of variations on a central motif, with echoing, stichomythic (single-line) exchanges contributing to the non-naturalistic, undifferentiated roles of characters occupying similar positions (cf. the repetitious utterances of Diana's nymphs and of the followers of Navarre). Opposing stances reveal the ambiguities inherent in the courses of action that the characters propose (cf. the debate between Galatea and Tityrus in *Galatea* 1.1, and Berowne's repudiation of the King's project in the opening scene of *Love's Labour's Lost*), while the attitudes of sub-plot characters challenge in both plays the assumed superior wisdom of authority figures.

The close relationship between the two works is most clearly apparent, however, in the structuring of Act 3 scene 1 of *Galatea* and Act 4 scene 3 of the Shakespearian play. In both scenes, a number of characters dedicated to a celibate condition enter in turn, reveal that they have fallen victim to love contrary to their oaths, and conceal themselves on the arrival of another, only to overhear a confession similar to their own. In both plays, the scene culminates with the emergence of the listeners from their place of concealment, a joint acknowledgement of their violation of their vows, and a recognition of the irresistible nature of the emotion by which they are gripped. The repetitious structure, with each character unaware of being overheard, is clearly is designed to evoke laughter through the superior knowledge of those outside the play world, but it simultaneously acts as a depersonalizing device, like the overt artifice and highly stylized nature of the works as a whole, subsuming each individual into a pattern of experience and a structure of ideas, rather than initiating the members of the audience into a specific condition or state of mind.

In *As You Like It*, by contrast, it is not his predecessor's skill in the formal structuring of an action through the use of parallel predicaments that is the primary focus of the later dramatist's attention but his handling of the emotional experience of those caught up in intractable positions. Though the influence of the Lylian comedy is again evident in much of the play, three scenes in particular seem to have lived in his imagination – 2.1, in which Galatea and Phillida encounter one another for the first time in their masculine roles, 3.2 in which the disguised girls seek to explore one another's feelings by 'supposing' themselves to be of the opposite sex, and 4.4 in which they guardedly express their love, and agree that one shall call the other 'Mistress'.[27]

In the first of these scenes no direct exchange between the characters in the Lylian drama takes place. Each expresses the desire to communicate with the other but is torn between her innate modesty and delicacy of mind and the assertiveness appropriate to her masculine role, and the encounter is interrupted before either can speak.[28] It is this tension, between the instinctive responses of the central figures and the imperatives of the roles they have elected to assume that Shakespeare takes up in the later play. Just as Galatea is troubled, for example, by the problem of matching her conduct to the expectations predicated by her male attire (cf. 'I would salute him, but I fear I should make a curtsy instead of a leg' and 'All the blood in my body would be in my face if he should ask me, as the question among men is common, "Are you a maid?"': 2.1.25–6 and 31–3), so Rosalind confesses that 'I could find in my heart to disgrace my man's apparel and to cry like a woman' (2.4.4–5), and is obliged to cover her swoon as a pretence when she falls into a faint on being presented with a blood-stained napkin (4.3.166–8). Like Phillida before her, Shakespeare's heroine urges herself into action with reminders of the way in which she is expected to behave (cf. 'But why stand I still? Boys should be bold': *Galatea*, 2.1.34; 'I must comfort the weaker vessel, as doublet and hose ought to show itself courageous to petticoat': *As You Like It*, 2.4.5–7), while

Rosalind's exclamation 'Dost thou think though I am caparisoned like a man I have a doublet and hose in my disposition' (3.2.191–3) echoes Galatea's reflections on the dichotomy between her female preferences and her dress (e.g. 'Blush, Galatea, that must frame thy affection fit for thy habit' (2.1.1–2).

The complex natures and situations of characters who simultaneously retain a feminine identity while acting out a masculine role, generating a species of epicene persona independent of either self, are elaborated in the central scenes of the Lylian play, and it is these ambiguities of personality and gender (ideally suited to performance by a boy actor), together with the predicaments to which they give rise, which Shakespeare develops. In 3.2 of *Galatea* each seeming youth invites the other to imagine 'him' to be a woman, propounding a hypothetical situation that will allow 'him' to test the other's feelings, while in 4.4 one proposes that the other should call 'him' 'mistress', permitting them to function as lovers on an imaginative level and enabling their otherwise inadmissible affection to 'have some show' (4.4.17–19). Similarly in 3.2 and 4.1 of the Shakespearian play, Ganymede's 'pretence' that 'he' is Rosalind and invitation to Orlando to woo 'him', is again a vehicle for emotional release, allowing both participants in the fiction a means for the exploration of uncharted emotions, and, in the case of the central character, an unwonted liberty of expression. The proposal that one disguised girl should call the other 'mistress' becomes, in the Shakespearian play, a betrothal between characters superficially of the same sex, in which both dramatis personae and audience engage in a complex negotiation between levels of reality, with those within the play world operating on different levels of understanding, and the ambivalences of a tentative wooing transmuted into a wedding that does and does not take place.

In *Twelfth Night*, by contrast, it is not the potential freedom from female constraints afforded by the process of 'supposing' but the restraints attendant upon gender exchange that Shakespeare takes up. Though at first sight Viola's situation might appear to look back to *As You Like It*, rather than to the sexual disguises of *Galatea*, it is clear from a number of verbal echoes, unparalleled elsewhere in the dramatist's work, that he returned not only to his own play but to the Lylian comedy from which it was ultimately derived. The riddling exchanges through which the central figures of the two plays both conceal and confide their female condition probably provide the most striking example:

INTRODUCTION

Phillida. Have you ever a sister?
Galatea. If I had but one, my brother must needs have two. But, I pray, have you ever a one?
Phillida. My father had but one daughter, and therefore I could have no sister.

(*Galatea*, 3.2.40–4)

Compare:

Viola. My father had a daughter lov'd a man,
  As it might be perhaps, were I a woman,
  I should your lordship.
. . .
Orsino. But died thy sister of her love, my boy?
Viola. I am all the daughters of my father's house,
  And all the brothers too: and yet I know not.
        (*Twelfth Night*, 2.4.108–22)

Once again, as in *As You Like It*, the complexities of situation and audience response afforded by gender disguise are the focus of the later dramatist's interest, but the tone of the work is very different from that of his previous realization of the potentialities inherent in the Lylian play. Just as Galatea and Phillida, having been obliged to adopt a masculine persona, find themselves locked in situations beyond their control and threatened with emotional attrition through their inability to communicate their love, so Viola, having adopted the role of Cesario, finds herself trapped in a position that she is unable to resolve (cf. 'O time, thou must untangle this, not I, / It is too hard a knot for me t'untie': 2.2.40–1), and able to express her feelings only by indirect means. Whereas Rosalind's disguise enables her to manipulate the outcome of events, Viola, like Galatea and Phillida before her, is released from the impasse in which she finds herself only by a wholly unforeseen turn of events, through which the two aspects of her epicene identity are enabled to glide miraculously apart (cf. Antonio's astonished enquiry, 'How have you made division of yourself' at 5.1.218, and Diana's wondering 'Is it possible?' (5.3.153) at the proposed metamorphosis of either Phillida or Galatea). The increasing distance in both plays between the desires of the characters and their capacity for emotional fulfilment lends a wistfulness to their exchanges without counterpart in either *As You Like It* or *Love's Labour's Lost*, epitomized by the 'supposings' of Lyly's disguised lovers and Viola's account of her hypothetical sister's fate (2.4.104–16).

Though few productions of Lyly's plays have taken place in modern times, both the dramatic structures that he designed and the predicaments that he explored have thus continued to be seen, in mutated form, in a wide variety of venues throughout the world. The Prologues and Epilogues to his works insistently affirm that signification is not an aspect of authorial intention but a product of audience response,[29] and it was in the imagination of the writer who was to succeed him as the principal luminary of the early modern stage that his ambivalent, malleable creations took on their most enduring forms.

GALATEA ON STAGE

Though an entry in the Stationers' Register (the mechanism through which copyright was secured in the sixteenth century) indicates that *Galatea* was in existence by 1585, there is no record of a production of the play prior to 1588 when it was performed on New Year's Day before the Queen. No account of that production survives, but the text, published in 1592, affords a significant amount of information on a variety of performance aspects of the work. The title-page announcement that the play was 'played before the Queen's Majesty at Greenwich, on New Year's day at night', indicates that it formed part of the revels, concentrated around the twelve days of Christmas (excluding Christmas Day itself), that took place annually at court between 1 November and the beginning of Lent. The fact that the play was performed at Greenwich (the monarch's favourite London residence) after nightfall implies that it took place in a banqueting hall by artificial light (cf. the wax 'torches' invoked in the Epilogue to *Campaspe*), and that the playing space was a relatively small one, permitting an intimate relationship between those inside and outside the play world.

Directions embedded in the dialogue afford further information regarding the staging of the work. Tityrus' allusions to 'this fair oak' at 1.1.2, and 'this tree' at 1.1.48 suggest that the tree to which the sacrificial virgin was destined to be bound was physically present on stage, and this suggestion is supported by the fact that trees figure in a number of Lyly's works,[30] and were among the properties known to be in the possession of the Office of the Revels.[31] The formulation 'where thou seest a heap of small pebble' at 1.1.15 implies that this too formed part of the set, testifying by its presence to the mutability of the play world (cf. the hacked remains of a felled tree in *Love's*

Metamorphosis, a play to which *Galatea* is closely related), while a pile of love-knots (possibly replacing the 'heap of small pebble') was patently needed in the second scene of Act 4 to enable Cupid to undertake the penance imposed on him by Diana.

A number of allusions supply information regarding the costumes with which the actors were supplied. References to the boy 'in the white coat' (e.g. at 3.1.46) imply that Galatea was dressed in a colour designed to denote her virgin condition; Peter's deduction that Dick is related to Rafe and Robin because of the nature of his coat (5.1.65–7) suggests that the three brothers were similarly clad; while Rafe's exclamation 'What black boy is this?' (2.3.8), heralding Peter's first entrance, signals that the Alchemist's apprentice was covered in something suggestive of soot. Similarly, Rafe's comment, 'This is a beggar', on encountering the Alchemist at 2.3.78, and his subsequent bewilderment at the discrepancy between the man's claims and the state of his clothes, points to the raggedness of the latter's condition, denoting the spuriousness of his 'art'.

Changes of costume and appearance are also charted by implied directions as the action evolves. Phillida departs, for example, at the close of 1.3 to disguise herself as a boy, and her references on her next appearance to the unfamiliarity of her garments (e.g. at 2.1.14–15) establish that she is now dressed in masculine attire. Cupid undergoes a series of metamorphoses subsequent to his first appearance in 1.2, signalled by Venus' exclamation at his changed appearance at 5.3.100–1: 'Alas, poor boy! Thy wings clipped? Thy brands quenched? Thy bow burnt, and thy arrows broke?' The lines indicate that prior to his decision to disguise himself he appeared as a winged boy, equipped with the torch, bow, and arrows traditionally associated with the god of love, only to be brought before Diana in chains subsequent to his capture, dressed as a bedraggled nymph, and finally appearing before the assembled gods in his own shape, but with the visual signifiers of his function broken or impaired.

Music and dancing also played a significant part in the theatrical event. A group of fairies with 'fair faces' (2.3.7) dance and play music in 2.3, offering a visual and aural contrast to the Alchemist's boy with his black face and ugly, incomprehensible speech. Robin, Rafe, and Dick sing together at the close of Act 1, and a further song is promised at the end of the play to mark the off-stage marriage of the central couple. The fact that the performers were boys, rather than adults (see pp. 14ff. above), suggests a sound-world remote from that of the twenty-first-century stage, combining with the slightness of build of the juvenile performers to create a delicate, exquisitely crafted effect. In all, the production was clearly designed to appeal to the ear and the eye as well as the mind, and to communicate by significant spectacle rather than by exclusively verbal means – and it is the stageability of the drama that has proved an enduring aspect of its appeal, consistently remarked upon by its recent directors.

No record of a further performance of the play survives from the early modern period, and few revivals of any of Lyly's works have taken place in recent times, though staged readings of the entire corpus, co-ordinated by James Wallace, have now taken place in London, in the 'Read Not Dead' series at the Education Department of Shakespeare's Globe. While some items in the corpus have no stage history whatsoever prior to their performance by the Read Not Dead troupe,[32] *Galatea* has fared rather better, and accounts of a range of productions, both amateur and professional, allow an insight into the motives prompting directorial choices in the staging of the work, and the problems encountered in the course of production. Four outdoor revivals are recorded by George K. Hunter in his Revels Edition of the play:[33] a 1905 production by the 'Idyllic Players' directed by Patrick Kirwan, on a 'grassy knoll beside the lake' in Regent's Park, which clearly focused on the pastoral aspects of the drama in that it formed part of a series of pastoral plays; a 1979 staging by the Apollo Society, directed by Michayel Pincombe, which took place in the grounds of St Catherine's College, Oxford, adjacent to the bank of the Cherwell River, and which enforced the dramatist's use of spectacle, with Neptune rising, festooned with weed, from the river in Act 5; a 1994 performance in the gardens of the Shakespeare Institute in Stratford-upon-Avon, directed by Emily Drugge; and a 1995 production at the University of New England, Armidale, New South Wales, Australia, directed by Professor Adrian Kernander, in which the use of boys for the roles of the mortals is indicative of an attempt to recapture the effect of a sixteenth-century performance of the work.[34]

Only one indoor revival (at the Roundhouse in London in 1976)[35] has been traced prior to the emergence of the new critical methodologies in the closing decades of the twentieth century (see pp. 29ff. below) that served to precipitate the play to the notice of a new generation of students and theatre practitioners.[36] At least eighteen productions have taken place between 1998 and 2011, including staged readings,[37] and the concepts governing the style of performance have been recorded in a number of cases. One of the earliest, directed by Kate D. Levin at Aaron Davis Hall in New York City in 1999,[38] is the subject of a substantial article, published in 2001, in which the director challenged the 'consensus that [Lyly's plays] are unproduceable', arguing that, in the case of *Galatea*, 'Lyly's text offers a highly satisfying blueprint for performance'.[39] Rather than seeking to recreate the experience of watching the work as first performed, her production strove to exhibit the inherent theatricality of the piece and its capacity to speak to a contemporary spectator. Cultural equivalents from the 1950s were evoked, for example, to resolve the problems posed by the concepts embodied in the classical deities (e.g. Neptune as a 'Sinatra-esque gangster': p. 31), while the distance between the human and divine spheres was signalled by the eighteenth-century costumes in which the mortals were dressed. Among a number of textual changes, the depersonalized nymphs of Diana were individualized, and their numbers expanded, while the 'unsatisfying ending' (p. 44) was replaced with an elaborate masque. In view of the number of cuts and interpolations, the production cannot be said to have exhibited that the text that has come down to us is an 'eminently theatrical script', but its success clearly confirmed the director's view that it is 'capable of being adapted to … the concerns and desires of present-day playgoers' (p. 28) – and it is the process of adaptation and modernization that has continued to inform the performance history of the work.

In the year prior to that in which Kate Levin's production took place, a group of students from Augustana College, Sioux Falls (South Dakota), produced the play under the direction of Ivan Fuller, anticipating Levin's handling of the work in a number of respects. Though the text was uncut, and sought to reproduce Elizabethan staging conditions with the audience on three sides and the playing space illuminated throughout, the action was interspersed with 1990s dance music, Cupid was dressed in silk boxer shorts, and the production was infused with broad humour designed to bring the comedy into the modern world. Similarly, a production of the play at the Théâtre des Ateliers by students from the University of Lyon, under the direction of Professor Francis Guinle, situated Elizabeth II (appropriately equipped with a handbag) rather than Elizabeth I on stage, while the apprentice mariners were assigned a dance in the first act reminiscent of the routine performed by the young sailors in Gene Kelly's *On the Town*.[40] An adaptation by Tim Browning in 2002, performed by the Quest Theater Ensemble, at Astoria, Queens, New York, was accompanied by music composed by a jazz guitarist (Spiros Exaras), while another New York production, by the Hangar Lab company (Ithaca) directed by Michelle Tattenbaum in 2003,[41] was founded upon 'a dedication to what is shockingly contemporary about Lyly's play, and a willingness to excise what is shockingly Elizabethan', embracing the need for scenes to be 'reordered ... split up and joined to other scenes to create a stronger sense of developing plot', and incorporating material from other plays by Lyly. The adapter's stated goal in shaping the play was not to 'make Lyly turn over in his grave' but to 'honor' a 'beautiful play', that delivered 'a powerful message' in 'celebrating love between two women', at a time 'when Americans [were] struggling to dictate the nature of marriage'.[42]

The fluidity of gender in the play world has inevitably inspired a number of productions, given the current focus of contemporary criticism. The workshops preceding a performance by Release the Hounds, a troupe of professional actors, in 2009, for example, explored notions of maturation, the role of social expectation in the determination of sexual behaviour, and the physiological proximity in Renaissance thought between female and male; [43] while a production at the University of California (Davis) in 2010, directed by Peter Lichtenfels, encouraged the audience to 'think about gender and sexuality' through a 'vaudeville style', that utilized live video, original music, outrageous costume, and text-messaging to enforce the contemporary resonances of the work. Yet more radically, the Stolen Chair Theatre company, under the direction of Jon Stancato, metamorphosed the drama (adapted by Kiran Rikhye) from a sophisticated sixteenth-century prose comedy into 'a racy contemporary blank verse play' entitled *The Stage Kiss* (New York, 2011), in which issues relating to gender definition were explored in a party atmosphere, to the accompaniment of instrumental versions of such un-Lylian songs as 'Girls Just Want to Have Fun';[44] while the Uncut Pages Theatre Company (Washington DC's Capitol Fringe Festival, 2007) produced the play with an all-female cast, reversing the circumstances of the original production, and bringing it emphatically into the modern world.[45]

The spate of revivals in recent years has not solely been a product, however, of the play's treatment of gender. The relationship of the work to a number of items in the Shakespearian canon, for example, clearly prompted its production at the American Shakespeare Center's Blackfriars' Playhouse in 2007, as part the week-long celebrations of Shakespeare's birthday,[46] and its inclusion in the Maryland Shakespeare Festival in 2009 (performed by a 'teen ensemble', Riotous Youth, and billed as 'Shakespeare's *Gallathea* ... Shakespeare before Shakespeare was Shakespeare'). Indeed, the extraordinary susceptibility of the work to a range of contemporary interpretations (and appropriations) is indicated by the varied personnel of three very recent productions and the markedly different experiences they have afforded spectators. In 2008, a troupe of boys from Kidbrooke School under the direction of Lucy Cuthbertson acted the play in the Painted Hall, Royal Naval College, Greenwich, recalling the first recorded performance of the piece, and thus recapturing some sense of the play as first produced; in 2011 a group of students from the English Department at Basel University, transformed the sound-world of the drama by the timbre of their voices, while emphatically locating the play in the modern era with a production promoted as 'Lyly's Disaster Comedy', overtly appealing to the contemporary taste for the untoward; while the play has now been launched into the technological arena in the form of a Lego version, 'John Lyly's *Gallathea* for Five Year Olds', on YouTube, taking the stylization of Lylian comedy to a new level, and considerably broadening the age-spectrum of the projected audience of the work.[47]

GALATEA AND ITS READERS

Though only one play by Lyly attracted a specific notice in his own age,[48] a number of comments on his work are indicative of the light in which his comedies were generally viewed. The term 'wit' (i.e. cleverness) is a constant motif in reflections on the Lylian corpus as a whole, while the commendatory letters prefacing the first collected edition of his plays in 1632 celebrate his originality ('the lyre he played on had no borrowed strings'), the subtlety of his compositions (his 'refined invention'), and his humour ('when old John Lyly is merry with thee in thy chamber, thou shalt say few or none of our poets [i.e. writers] now are such witty companions').[49] Though his reputation declined in the early seventeenth century, he was one of the first of the early modern dramatists to receive significant critical attention following the revival of interest in the work of Shakespeare's contemporaries at the start of the nineteenth century, and all his plays had appeared in print by 1868, attracting favourable notice from some of the foremost writers and critics of the age.[50] It was the monumental, three-volume, critical edition of the entire

Lylian canon by R. Warwick Bond in 1902, however, that laid the foundations for the scholarly exploration of the dramatist's work. Though the assumptions underlying much of Bond's critical material now seem ludicrously outdated (e.g. his contention that Lyly's 'proudest achievement' was 'to render in her wonted speech and fashion that inconstant gleam, that dancing firefly, the English girl'),[51] his text remains a major point of reference for any new edition of the plays, while the topics he explored – the dating of the works, the use of euphuistic prose, the treatment of source materials, the structuring of the plots, and influence on Shakespeare – continued to inform Lylian studies for much of the twentieth century. His summary of the dramatist's distinction as 'the cleverest, with the possible exception of [Jonson] the most learned, and in spite of that the most modern of [Shakespeare's contemporaries]'[52] forges a fascinating link, moreover, between the sixteenth-century location of 'wit' as the primary characteristic of the Lylian corpus and the sense of modernity registered by recent critics and theatre practitioners in encountering the work.

The mid-twentieth century witnessed a shift away from the character-orientated criticism typified by Bond. In his *John Lyly: The Humanist as Courtier* (1962), a book widely regarded as laying the foundations for modern Lylian studies, G. K. Hunter argued that 'By using a critical vocabulary which does not import assumptions that the end of drama is to develop characters, organize intrigue and show personality at work, we take ourselves a little nearer the true excellencies of Lyly's plays' (p. 199) – and that contention was justified by the emergence, in the third quarter of the twentieth century, by a range of fresh approaches to the work. In a ground-breaking article published in 1958,[53] Jonas Barish demonstrated that the euphuistic mode, as used by Lyly, was the vehicle not for the precise articulation of ideas but for the location of a pervasive ambivalence informing every aspect of experience (see pp. 3–4 above); while a widespread shift of emphasis in critical discourse from character to structure was evidenced in M. C. Bradbrook's assertion that the procedures of Lylian drama are analogous to those of 'a perspective puzzle with cubes or pyramids' in that 'any visual reading may be reversed'.[54] Predictably, in the light of the critical position quoted above, Hunter's own analysis of *Galatea* was also conducted in very different in terms from those employed by Bond. Though attentive to the play's 'evocation of refined attitudes', leading to a fuller understanding of 'what sensitivity and delicacy are' (pp. 200 and

203), his analysis focused not upon nuances of character but on the quasi-musical structuring of the plot, and the creation of 'one of the most beautifully articulated plays in the period' through a process analogous to the composition of a fugue (p. 198). An edition of *Galatea* and *Midas* by Anne Lancashire in 1969[55] moved still further, moreover, from the early twentieth-century concern with individualized experience, arguing that 'characters are important not as human individuals but as fixed representations of different moral points of view' (p. xxiv), and that *Galatea* emerges, when read in this light, as a highly complex debate on the nature of love, typical in its 'ironic complexity' of the 'extraordinary toughness and depth of Lyly's plays' (p. xxvii).

A remarkable period of Lylian scholarship was brought to a close, in the same year in which Anne Lancashire's edition appeared, with the publication of Peter Saccio's *The Court Comedies of John Lyly* (Princeton, NJ), a book that remains a major landmark in the criticism of Lyly's work. Once again, the discussion of *Galatea* stressed the 'mathematical' structuring of the play, and the way in which 'juxtaposed scenes create a series of internal echoes, parallels, and balanced contrasts that dance forward with expanded meaning and rhythm' (p. 160), but it departed from the work of previous commentators by the contention that it is not the amatory instinct but the attempted defiance of divinity that underlies all the drama's events. Where Lancashire, for example, argued that *Galatea* 'is a play about the nature of love, and how it physically and mentally affects man' (p. xxiv), Saccio saw the forward movement of the action as 'the exfoliation of the central figures of the gods', whose values are progressively unfolded through the 'resonating echoes' of the classical myths evoked by the dramatist in the course of the work (p. 160).

The emergence of new critical methodologies in the closing decades of the twentieth century opened a yet wider range of fresh perspectives on the plays. My own *The Metamorphosis of 'Gallathea': A Study in Creative Adaptation*, still the only book-length study of the work (see n. 26), sought to exhibit its pervasive ambivalence, and to chart a series of intertextual interactions between the play and a number of items in the Shakespearian canon. An interest in Lylian drama in performance, heralded in the mid-1960s with the work of Michael Best,[56] burgeoned into explorations of the play in relation to the culture of the Elizabethan court,[57] a greater emphasis on the dramatist's use of spectacle,[58] and on the text as a blueprint for performance on both the sixteenth-century and the contemporary stage.[59] It is the twin topics of politics and gender, however, that have undoubtedly dominated critical discussions of the plays in recent years. The two interrelated strands of contemporary discourse were drawn together in Michael Pincombe's *The Plays of John Lyly: Eros and Eliza*,[60] which explored the 'counter-courtly' aspects of Lyly's work, and the 'glimmerings of ... disaffection' (p. 139) with the cult of the virgin monarch evidenced in *Galatea*; while a host of studies devoted to such issues as whether the same-sex love between Lyly's maidens implies homoeroticism, a validation of virginal autonomy, or a transgressive rebellion against the divine have served to establish the play as a central text for the exploration of the representation of gender on the early modern stage. A full account of the range of contributions to the field is beyond the scope of this introduction, but the breadth of interest in the subject is evidenced by Denise A. Walen's article 'Constructions of Female Homoerotics in Early Modern Drama',[61] which argues that *Galatea* is of particular interest for gender studies in that it is the female characteristics of the central couple, rather than their masculine appearance, that attracts the disguised maidens to one another; Valerie Traub's 'The Renaissance of Lesbianism in Early Modern England',[62] contending that the play 'reproduces social orthodoxy' but nevertheless 'gestures towards the enactment of erotic passion for one's own sex' (p. 252); and Christopher Wixson's 'Cross-Dressing and John Lyly's *Gallathea*',[63] which seeks to bring together social and sexual transgression, arguing that the play is 'an elaborate illustration of social stratification and privilege that, via a complex manipulation of audience sympathy ... legitimates the power of the ruler and the order of the realm' (p. 245). For all the widespread interest in the field, however, the relevance of some twentieth- and twenty-first-century gender studies to dramatic practice on the early modern stage has not been universally endorsed. George K. Hunter, for example, in his turn-of-the-century Revels edition of the play, expressed doubts that 'the theatrical conventions of the period (particularly those that attach to boy players of female roles) enable us to open up the unarticulated social and psychological attitudes of the time' (Hunter, p. 24, n. 20), while Wixson warns against an over exclusive focus on gender or sexual subversions at the expense of 'the larger social project' of individual plays (p. 242).

In a discussion of Lyly's *Endymion* in 1975, Joseph Houppert declared, '*Endimion* [*sic*] is Lyly's *Hamlet*. No historical or allegorical approach satisfies more than a few critics; the ending shrouds the play in ambiguity; and there are so many fashionable topics that every man finds something of interest'.[64] Fanciful though the comparison with *Hamlet* might seem at first sight, the comment might well be applied to *Galatea*. While being deeply embedded in the cultural forms of its own age, and overtly directed towards the immediate concerns of a specific court, the work has continued to speak to the interests of successive generations of readers (as the eco-criticism with which this introduction opened confirms), affording a final testimony, in its paradoxical remoteness and modernity, its mathematical precision and open-endedness, to the insistent ambiguity that constitutes the hallmark of the dramatist's work.

THIS EDITION AND THE EDITORIAL HISTORY OF THE PLAY

Galatea appeared in two early editions (1592 and 1632) and is among the more frequently edited of Lyly's plays in modern times. A lightly annotated old-spelling edition was published by F. W. Fairholt in his two-volume *The Dramatic Works of John Lilly* in 1858, and this was succeeded in 1902 by R. Warwick Bond's much more extensively annotated old-spelling edition in his three-volume collection of Lyly's complete prose and dramatic works, which laid the foundations, as noted above (pp. 27–28), for modern Lylian studies. A series of modern-spelling editions followed in the course of the twentieth century, all designed to introduce the work to students and to make it accessible to the general reader: Anne Lancashire's '*Gallathea*' and '*Midas*' (see p. 29 above), which includes a helpful introduction and informative notes; Russell A. Fraser and Norman Rabkin's *Drama of the English Renaissance*, vol. i (New York, 1976), locating the work in the context of a spectrum of sixteenth-century plays; Carter A. Daniel's *The Plays of John Lyly* (Lewisburg, 1988), a lightly annotated collection overtly designed to counter Lyly's neglect; and my own *John Lyly Selected Prose and Dramatic Works* (Manchester, 1997, reprinted New York, 2003), positioning the play in relation to other items in the Lylian canon. A photo-facsimile of the first edition of the play, with a detailed bibliographical introduction, has also appeared, published by The Malone Society (Oxford, 1998).[65]

Though all the works noted above have been consulted in the preparation of this edition, it is to George K. Hunter's text of the

play in the Revels Plays series that it primarily looks back. A new
introduction and fresh explanatory notes have been supplied,
however, in line with the requirements of the Revels Students Editions series, and some minor changes (e.g. to some stage directions)
have been introduced. In line with all modern editions of Lyly's
plays, the songs, omitted from the Lylian quartos,[66] but included in
Blount's collected edition of 1632 (see p. 3. n.3 above), have been
incorporated into the text. All other departures from the first edition
are signalled by square brackets.

NOTES

1 The current spelling of the title was introduced by George K. Hunter in
his Revels edition of the play as more etymologically correct than the
earlier version. See George K. Hunter and David Bevington (eds),
Galatea: Midas, Revels Plays (Manchester, 2000), p. 28, n. 2.

2 Cf. Phillida's resolve to ground her conduct on social expectation: 'But
why stand I still? Boys should be bold' (2.1.34).

3 The term is drawn from the encomium on Lyly's work prefacing *Six
Court Comedies*, the first collected edition of the dramatist's work, published by Edward Blount in 1632. Blount writes: 'Our nation are in his
debt for a new English which he taught them. *Euphues and His England*
began first that language. All our ladies were then his scholars, and that
beauty in court which could not parley Euphuism was as little regarded
as she which now there speaks not French' (quoted from R. Warwick
Bond, *The Complete Works of John Lyly*, vol. 3 (Oxford, 1902, reprinted
1973), p. 3. Spelling and punctuation have been modernized for the
purposes of this edition).

4 The place of education is significant in that, though it was usual for
both the study and performance of plays to occupy a significant place in
the school curriculum at this time, documentary evidence (and the fact
that Marlowe also attended the King's School) suggests that the role
played by drama in the Canterbury syllabus was particularly strong. See
G. K. Hunter, *John Lyly: The Humanist as Courtier* (London, 1962), pp.
38–9.

5 See his accusation in the letter 'To My Very Good Friends the Gentlemen
Scholars of Oxford', introduced into the second edition of his first published work (*Euphues: The Anatomy of Wit*) in which he complains that
he was given 'bones to gnaw before I could get the teat to suck ... and
was, at the last, enforced to wean myself' (quoted from Leah Scragg, ed.,
'Euphues: The Anatomy of Wit' and 'Euphues and His England', Revels Plays
Companion Library series (Manchester, 2003, p. 151). All subsequent
references to the two parts of *Euphues* are to this edition.

6 Works overtly indebted to *Euphues* or designed to capitalize upon its
success include Greene's *Euphues, his Censure of Philautus* (1587) and
Lodge's *Rosalynde* (1590), itself the source of Shakespeare's *As You
Like It*.

7 See Blount's encomium on Lyly's work, quoted in n. 2 above.

8 Cf. Euphues' reflection that love is 'like the apple tree in Persia, whose blossom savoureth like honey, whose bud is more sour than gall' (p. 54), and Eubulus' reminder to Euphues that 'the sweetest wine turneth to the sharpest vinegar' (p. 37).

9 The term is drawn from Jonas A. Barish, 'The Prose Style of John Lyly', *English Literary History*, 23 (1956), pp. 14–35, reprinted in Ruth Lunney (ed.), *John Lyly* (Farnham, 2011), pp. 49–70. The article laid the foundations for the study of euphuism in the modern period and remains the most perceptive analysis of the style.

10 *Love's Metamorphosis*, which looks back to bk viii of Ovid's *Metamorphoses*. For a detailed discussion of the relationship between this play and Ovid's work, see Leah Scragg, ed., *Love's Metamorphosis*, Revels Plays (Manchester, 2008).

11 Unless otherwise stated, all references to Ovid's *Metamorphoses* are to volume ii of the Loeb edition, translated by Frank Justus Miller, revised G. P. Goold (Cambridge, Mass., 1984).

12 See Arthur Golding, 'Epistle to the Right Honourable ... Earl of Leicester', *The xv Books of P. Ovidius Naso, entitled 'Metamorphosis'* (1567), lines 10–12 (spelling and punctuation of both title and quotation have been modernized for the purposes of this edition).

13 Lyly's indebtedness to Ovid is evident in the proximity between Tityrus' lengthy description of the changing landscape of the play (*Galatea*, 1.1.15ff.) and a number of passages of the Latin work (cf. Ovid's account of the way in which the angry Poseidon 'flooded the country till it looked like a sea, swept away the farmers' crops and overwhelmed their fields beneath their waters' (*Metamorphoses*, xi, 208–10, p. 135).

14 *John Lyly: The Humanist as Courtier*, p. 60.

15 The conflict between Octavius Caesar and the combined forces of Brutus and Cassius.

16 Compare the title-page announcement that Lyly's fourth play, *Endymion*, was performed 'Before the Queen's Majesty at Greenwich, at Candlemas Day at night'.

17 See Bond, vol. i, pp. 477–84. A number of other entertainments provided for the Queen may be found in the same volume.

18 Numerous non-dramatic literary compositions also celebrated the sovereign in terms either directly or tangentially related to the pastoral tradition. See, for example, the April eclogue of Spenser's *Shepherd's Calendar* (1579).

19 The exception is a late play, *Mother Bombie*, performed at the playhouse in St Paul's Cathedral.

20 Even in this play, however, an unswerving refusal to love is questioned through the figure of Sibylla, who functions as the shadowy obverse of the monarch of the play.

21 See the comment by Rosencrantz in *Hamlet* (2.2.342–5) that a troupe of child actors 'are now the fashion, and so berattle the common stages – so they call them – that many ... dare scarce come thither' (quoted from Richard Proudfoot, Ann Thompson, and David Scott Kastan (eds), *The Arden Shakespeare Complete Works* (London, 1998, rev. 2001). All subsequent references to Shakespeare's plays are to this edition).

22 In *Galatea*, for example, the cast is made up of ten women (cf. the very small number of female roles on the 'public' stage), five boys, an unspecified number of fairies, two members of the local community of indeterminate age, and only eight adult men, none of whose relatively small parts is beyond the capabilities of an older boy.

23 All references to *Sappho and Phao* are to the edition by David Bevington, published with *Campaspe* (ed. George K. Hunter) in 1991 in the Revels Plays series.

24 See the Epistle prefacing *Wits miserie, and the worlds madnesse* (1596).

25 *Palladis Tamia* (1598).

26 For a detailed account of the relationship between the play and the Shakespearian corpus, see Leah Scragg, *The Metamorphosis of 'Gallathea': A Study in Creative Adaptation* (Washington DC, 1982). Of the other Shakespearian plays that draw on Lyly's work the most significant, in terms of its degree of indebtedness, is *A Midsummer Night's Dream*.

27 It should be noted here that Shakespeare's indebtedness to Lyly in this play is more complicated than in *Love's Labour's Lost*, in that the principal source of the work, Lodge's *Rosalynde*, itself looks back to *Galatea*. There is considerable evidence to suggest, however, that Shakespeare returned directly to the Lylian play, rather than simply re-encountering it second-hand.

28 Though the attitudes in question might be regarded as socially constructed in the twenty-first century, the term 'innate' is used here in that they were thought to be God-given (and thus in-born) when the play was composed.

29 The Epilogue at the Blackfriars in *Campaspe*, for example, declares that 'Our exercises must be as your judgement is, resembling water, which is always of the same colour into what it runneth' (lines 4–6), while the Prologue to *Galatea* asserts that 'as in the ground where gold groweth nothing will prosper but gold, so in Your Majesty's mind, where nothing doth harbour but virtue, nothing can enter but virtue' (lines 15–18).

30 Cf. the on-stage release of Bagoa from an arborified state in *Endymion* and the felling of a tree dedicated to Ceres in *Love's Metamorphosis*.

31 The office responsible for supplying scenery, properties, and costumes for entertainments at court.

32 *Love's Metamorphosis*, for example, has no recorded stage history, and no performance of *Sappho and Phao* is known to have taken place between 1584 and 2007 when it was performed, under the direction of Andy Kesson, at the Shakespeare Institute in Stratford.

33 All information on the following four productions, including the quoted material, is derived from Hunter's edition.

34 Hunter notes (p. 21) in relation to this production, 'A videotape of two scenes … makes it clear how well Lyly's diction is suited to boys' voices and to the slightly disengaged manner of their performance'.

35 Performed by students from the University of St Andrews.

36 I am indebted to a number of scholars and theatre practitioners for information on the following productions, notably Dr Sue Hall-Smith who researched the theatre history of the play on my behalf.

37 Both Primavera Productions, directed by Tom Littler (King's Head Theatre, London), and the Read Not Dead troupe, co-ordinated by

James Wallace (Education Department of Shakespeare's Globe), mounted staged readings in 2007, while the latter production was later revived at the Queen's House, Greenwich, in 2010.

38 The play was produced under the auspices of the Theatre Program of the City College of New York (CUNY).

39 Kate D. Levin, 'Playing with Lyly; Theatrical Criticism and Non-Shakespearian Drama', *Research Opportunities in Renaissance Drama*, 40 (2001), pp. 25–53, reprinted in Lunney (ed.), *John Lyly*, pp. 461–89. The passages quoted are from p. 26 (Lunney, p. 462).

40 I am indebted to Hunter's edition of the play in the Revels Plays series for information regarding this production.

41 The production was subsequently revived at the HERE Arts Center, NY, in 2004.

42 All quotations regarding the adapter's stance towards the project are drawn from the director's website.

43 The play was performed at the Pleasaunce Theatre Islington (London) in 2009, following a series of workshops and the presentation of extracts at the Bridewell Theatre.

44 All information regarding this production is derived from Ed Malin's review in the nytheatre.com archive.

45 The production is of particular interest in that it was staged by a group of students from the same college (Bryn Mawr) as the troupe which performed Lyly's *The Woman in the Moon* in 1928, with Katherine Hepburn (then a student at the college) in the title role.

46 Directed by Brett Sullivan Santry and performed by the students of Stuart Hall School (Staunton, Virginia), the production sought to recapture aspects of a sixteenth-century performance of the work through, for example, an emphasis on the patterned nature of the dramatic language, cross-gender casting, universal lighting, and an intimate audience–actor relationship.

47 The action is accompanied by a narration that might prove taxing to the infant mind, while some elements of the drama are somewhat confused (e.g. the identification of the Augur with the Agar).

48 *Mother Bombie*, used by Thomas Nashe as a measure of hilarity in an attack on Gabriel Harvey in his *Have with you to Saffron-Walden* (1596).

49 Quoted from Bond, i, pp. 2 and 3. Spelling and punctuation have been modernized for the purposes of this edition.

50 See F. W. Fairholt, *The Dramatic Works of John Lilly* (1586), vol. i, p. xxiii. Fairholt cites Malone, Hazlitt, and Lamb, for example, among Lyly's admirers.

51 Vol. ii, p. 283.

52 Vol. ii, p. 299.

53 See n. 9 above.

54 *The Growth and Structure of Elizabethan Drama* (London, 1955), p. 62.

55 Regents Renaissance Drama series (University of Nebraska Press).

56 Cf. 'The Staging and Production of the Plays of John Lyly', *Theatre Research*, 9, pp. 104–17.

57 Cf. Anne Lancashire, 'John Lyly and Pastoral Entertainment', *The Elizabethan Theatre*, VIII (1982), pp. 22–50.

58 Cf. Leah Scragg, 'Speaking Pictures: Style and Spectacle in Lylian Comedy', *English Studies*, 86 (2005), pp. 298–311, reprinted in Lunney (ed.), *John Lyly*, pp. 413–26.

59 See, for example, Kent Cartwright, 'The Confusions of *Gallathea*: John Lyly as Popular Dramatist', *Comparative Drama*, 32 (1998), pp. 207–39, reprinted in Lunney (ed.), *John Lyly*, pp. 427–59, and Kate D. Levin, 'Playing With Lyly', discussed on p. 25 above.

60 Revels Plays Companion Library series (Manchester, 1996).

61 *Theatre Journal*, 54 (2002), pp. 411–30, reprinted in Lunney (ed.), *John Lyly*, pp. 331–50.

62 *GLQ, A Journal of Lesbian and Gay Studies*, 7 (2001), pp. 245–63.

63 *Studies in English Literature, 1500–1900*, 41 (2001), pp. 241–56, reprinted in Lunney (ed.), *John Lyly*, pp. 351–66.

64 *John Lyly*, Twaine's English Authors series (Boston, 1975), p. 96.

65 Ed., Leah Scragg.

66 I.e. the first published editions of Lyly's plays.

GALATEA

Characters in Order of Appearance

TITYRUS, *a shepherd.*
GALATEA, *his daughter.*
CUPID, *youthful god of love, son to Venus.*
NYMPH, *a follower of Diana.*
MELIBEUS, *a shepherd.*   5
PHILLIDA, *his daughter.*
ROBIN,
RAFE,   } *three brothers, sons of a miller.*
DICK,
A MARINER.   10
DIANA, *goddess of chastity and the hunt.*
TELUSA,
EUROTA, } *followers (nymphs) of Diana.*
RAMIA,

---

1. *TITYRUS*] a name derived from Virgil's First Eclogue, a pastoral poem
in which a shepherd and a goatherd compare the condition of their lives (cf.
MELIBEUS at line 5 below). The first lines of the Eclogue are echoed at the
start of 1.1, furthering the association between the two works.

2. *GALATEA*] Denoting 'milk-white', and literalized in the 'white coat' in
which the play's title-figure is dressed (cf. 3.1.46, 3.1.67), the name implies
the character's virgin condition. Like *Tityrus* and *Melibeus* the name occurs
in Virgil's First Eclogue (see lines 1 and 5nn.), but its use also invites association with the Galatea of classical myth, a sea-nymph pursued by the Cyclops,
Polyphemus.

5. *MELIBEUS*] The name of one of the two speakers in Virgil's First
Eclogue (see lines 1 and 2nn. above), reinforcing the link between the two
works, and the pastoral location of the play.

6. *PHILLIDA*] Etymologically related to Phyllis, the name hints at the
transformations endemic in the play world, in that the Phyllis of classical
myth was changed into an almond tree.

7, 8, 9. *ROBIN, RAFE, DICK*] As sons of a miller (see 5.1.65–76) the boys
are associated with a readiness to cheat, in that millers were notorious for giving
short measure by pressing down the scales with their thumbs (see 2.3.141–2n.).

12, 13, 14. *TELUSA, EUROTA, RAMIA*] all names with classical origins
and evocative of the pastoral location in which the action is set. *Telusa* recalls
Telus, the Roman goddess of the earth, and may also be designed to suggest
Latin *telum*, a dart or spear, a weapon appropriate to a nymph devoted to the

39

NEPTUNE, *god of the sea, supreme deity of the play.*   15
FAIRIES.
PETER, *servant to an Alchemist.*
AN ALCHEMIST.
AN ASTRONOMER.
LARISSA, *another nymph of Diana.*   20
AN AUGUR.
Two countrymen of the shepherds.
ERICTHINIS, *another countryman of the shepherds.*
HEBE, *a virgin.*
VENUS, *goddess of love.*   25

SCENE: *the bank of the river Humber and adjacent woods.*

---

pleasures of the hunt. *Eurota* is derived from *Eurotas*, a major water course in
Sparta, and is thus in tune with the riverine setting of the work, while *Ramia*
(derived from Latin *ramis*, a branch) suggests the woods in which much of the
action takes place.

17. *PETER*] The name may be derived from the exclamation 'Peter!' (an
abbreviated form of 'By Saint Peter') which occurs in the source (Chaucer's
'The Canon's Yeoman's Tale') from which Lyly's alchemical material derives.

18. *ALCHEMIST*] a type of experimental scientist, professing the ability
to turn base metals into gold. Alchemy was still regarded by many in the
sixteenth century as a legitimate science.

19. *ASTRONOMER*] one claiming to be able to read the future through
the position of the stars (cf. modern English 'astrologer').

20. *LARISSA*] a name usually signifying a daughter of the earliest inhabitants of ancient Greece in classical mythology, but possibly designed here to
recall 'Larissus', a river flowing into the Ionian sea (cf. the pastoral associa-
tions of *TELUSA, EUROTA* and *RAMIA* at lines 12, 13, and 14nn. above).

21. *AUGUR*] technically, a Roman religious official who foretold the
future on the basis of omens deduced from natural phenomena, but used
here more broadly as one charged with the organization of a religious rite.

23. *ERICTHINIS*] a name derived from a Latin term denoting something
pertaining to a specific community, and thus signifying here a member of
the people.

24. *HEBE*] the Roman name for the goddess of youth, used here to
emphasize the horror of the premature death threatening an innocent young
woman.

26. Humber] a long estuary dividing the counties of Lincolnshire and
Yorkshire on the east coast of England.

The Prologue

Ios and Smyrna were two sweet cities, the first named of the violet, the latter of the myrrh: Homer was born in the one and buried in the other. Your Majesty's judgement and favour are our sun and shadow, the one coming of your deep wisdom, the other of your wonted grace. We in all humility desire that   5
by the former receiving our first breath we may in the latter take our last rest.

Augustus Caesar had such piercing eyes that whoso looked on him was constrained to wink; Your Highness hath so perfect a judgement that whatsoever we offer we are   10
enforced to blush. Yet as the Athenians were most curious that the lawn wherewith Minerva was covered should be without spot or wrinkle, so have we endeavoured with all care that

---

1–3. *Ios . . . other*] Ios (an island in the Aegean sea) and Smyrna (modern Ismir) are the traditional sites of the birth (Smyrna) and burial (Ios) of the Greek epic poet Homer. The two are linked as *sweet cities* by the fact that their names carry connotations of fragrance (*Ios* = Gk violet: *Smyrna* = Gk myrhh).

4. *our sun and shadow*] that which gives us life and our source of protection.

the one] the light of your approval.

5. *the other*] the security afforded by your favourable notice.

wonted] customary.

6–7. *by the former . . . rest*] having been initially encouraged in our endeavours by your judiciousness, we may rely at the last on your generosity of mind.

8–9. *Augustus . . . wink*] a traditional story regarding the penetrating gaze of the Emperor Augustus, related by the Roman historian Suetonius.

9. *wink*] close his eyes.

11. *curious*] particular.

12–13. *the lawn . . . wrinkle*] a reference to the *peplus*, a robe woven annually for the statue of the Greek goddess Athene (Roman Minerva). The reference to Minerva (goddess of wisdom) is appropriate in this context in that Elizabeth was frequently equated with her by virtue of her acuteness of mind.

12. *lawn*] fine linen.

what we present Your Highness should neither offend in scene
nor syllable, knowing that as in the ground where gold groweth   15
nothing will prosper but gold, so in Your Majesty's mind,
where nothing doth harbour but virtue, nothing can enter but
virtue.

14–15. *should neither . . . syllable*] should not give offence through either
that which is enacted or said.

15–16. *knowing that . . . gold*] a traditional belief, recorded by the Roman
natural historian Pliny, that gold-bearing land is infertile.

15. *groweth*] abounds.

17. *doth harbour*] resides.

Act 1

[*Enter*] TITYRUS [*and*] GALATEA
              [*disguised as a boy, with a white coat*].

Tityrus. The sun doth beat upon the plain fields; wherefore
    let us sit down, Galatea, under this fair oak, by whose
    broad leaves being defended from the warm beams we
    may enjoy the fresh air, which softly breathes from
    Humber floods.   [*They sit down under the tree.*]   5
Galatea. Father, you have devised well, and whilst our flock
    doth roam up and down this pleasant green you shall
    recount to me, if it please you, for what cause this tree
    was dedicated unto Neptune, and why you have thus
    disguised me.   10
Tityrus. I do agree thereto, and when thy state and my care
    be considered, thou shalt know this question was not
    asked in vain.
Galatea. I willingly attend.
Tityrus. In times past, where thou seest a heap of small pebble,   15
    stood a stately temple of white marble, which was dedi-
    cated to the god of the sea (and in right, being so near
    the sea). Hither came all such as either ventured by long

---

    0.2. with a white coat] See 3.1.46 and 67 for evidence of the costume in
which Galatea is dressed. For the significance of the colour of her coat, see
Characters in Order of Appearance, line 2n.
    1–5.] an echo of the opening lines of Virgil's First Eclogue (see Characters
in Order of Appearance, lines 1, 2, and 5nn.), reinforcing the pastoral setting
of the play.
    1. *plain*] open.
    5. *Humber floods*] the waters of the Humber (an estuary on the east coast
of England). See Characters in Order of Appearance, line 26n.
    6. *devised well*] made a good proposal.
    11. *state*] predicament.
    17. *in right*] properly so.
    18–19. *ventured . . . countries*] dared to undertake long voyages in order to
see other lands.

travel to see countries or by great traffic to use merchandise, offering sacrifice by fire to get safety by water, yield-   20
ing thanks for perils past and making prayers for good
success to come. But Fortune, constant in nothing but
inconstancy, did change her copy as the people their
custom; for the land being oppressed by Danes, who
instead of sacrifice committed sacrilege, instead of religion   25
rebellion, and made a prey of that in which they should
have made their prayers, tearing down the temple even
with the earth, being almost equal with the skies, enraged
so the god who binds the winds in the hollows of the earth
that he caused the seas to break their bounds sith men   30
had broke their vows, and to swell as far above their reach
as men had swerved beyond their reason. Then might you
see ships sail where sheep fed, anchors cast where ploughs
go, fishermen throw their nets where husbandmen sow
their corn, and fishes throw their scales where fowls do   35
breed their quills. Then might you gather froth where now
is dew, rotten weeds for sweet roses, and take view of
monstrous mermaids instead of passing fair maids.

19–20. *by great . . . merchandise*] to engage in commerce through the
extensive trading of goods.

22–3. *constant . . . inconstancy*] a proverbial expression, reiterated in a
variety of forms throughout the Lylian corpus, and central to the dramatist's
vision of an unstable world.

23–4. *did change . . . custom*] altered her course when people changed their
behaviour.

24–8. *for the land . . . skies*] The east coast of England was subject to a
series of raids by Vikings (Danes) between the eighth and early eleventh
centuries, with religious establishments being a particular focus of attack.
The reference to the Danish invasions contributes to the conflation of historical periods at work in the play. See Introduction, pp. 9–10.

27. *even*] level.

28. *being*] having been.

29. *so*] to such an extent.

the god . . . earth] Neptune, creator of storms at sea, rather than Aeolus,
god of the winds.

30. *sith*] since.

31. *reach*] usual limits.

34. *husbandmen*] farmers.

35–6. *fowls . . . quills*] birds grow their feathers.

38. *mermaids*] hybrid beings, part women part fish (hence their description as *monstrous* in the same line), credited with luring mariners to

Galatea. To hear these sweet marvels I would mine eyes were
    turned also into ears.   40
Tityrus. But at the last, our countrymen repenting, and not
    too late because at last, Neptune, either weary of his
    wrath or wary to do them wrong, upon condition con-
    sented to ease their miseries.
Galatea. What condition will not miserable men accept?   45
Tityrus. The condition was this: that at every five years' day,
    the fairest and chastest virgin in all the country should
    be brought unto this tree, and here being bound (whom
    neither parentage shall excuse for honour, nor virtue for
    integrity) is left for a peace-offering unto Neptune.   50
Galatea. Dear is the peace that is bought with guiltless blood.
Tityrus. I am not able to say that; but he sendeth a monster
    called the Agar, against whose coming the waters roar,
    the fowls fly away, and the cattle in the field for terror
    shun the banks.   55
Galatea. And she bound to endure that horror?
Tityrus. And she bound to endure that horror.
Galatea. Doth this monster devour her?
Tityrus. Whether she be devoured of him, or conveyed to
    Neptune, or drowned between both, it is not permitted   60
    to know, and incurreth danger to conjecture. Now,
    Galatea, here endeth my tale and beginneth thy tragedy.
Galatea. Alas, father, and why so?

---

destruction through the beauty of their song. Modern spelling (cf. the 'Mare-
maides' of the 1592 edition) obscures the rhyme with *fair maids* at line 38.
    passing] unsurpassably.
    46. *five years' day*] on a particular day, every five years.
    48–50. *whom neither . . . integrity*] who shall not be exempt on the grounds
of either the importance of her family or the virtue of her own uncorrupted
course of life.
    53. *Agar*] a personification of the 'eagre', the tidal bore (i.e. surge of water
of unusual height) occurring periodically in the Humber estuary.
    against whose coming] in anticipation of whose arrival.
    54. *fowls*] birds.
    56. *bound*] obliged.
    57. *bound*] physically restrained, tied.
    59. *of*] by.
    61. *incurreth . . . conjecture*] jeopardizes one's safety to speculate.

Tityrus. I would thou hadst been less fair or more fortunate,
then shouldst thou not repine that I have disguised thee in   65
this attire; for thy beauty will make thee to be thought
worthy of this god. To avoid, therefore, destiny (for wisdom
ruleth the stars), I think it better to use an unlawful means,
your honour preserved, than intolerable grief, both life and
honour hazarded, and to prevent, if it be possible, thy   70
constellation by my craft. Now hast thou heard the custom
of this country, the cause why this tree was dedicated unto
Neptune, and the vexing care of thy fearful father.

Galatea. Father, I have been attentive to hear and, by your
patience, am ready to answer. Destiny may be deferred,   75
not prevented; and therefore it were better to offer myself
in triumph than to be drawn to it with dishonour. Hath
Nature (as you say) made me so fair above all, and shall
not Virtue make me as famous as others? Do you not
know, or doth over-carefulness make you forget, that an   80
honourable death is to be preferred before an infamous
life? I am but a child, and have not lived long, and yet
not so childish as I desire to live ever. Virtues I mean to
carry to my grave, not grey hairs. I would I were as sure
that destiny would light on me as I am resolved it could   85
not fear me. Nature hath given me beauty; Virtue courage:
Nature must yield me death; Virtue honour. Suffer me,

65. *repine*] regret.
67–8. *To avoid . . . stars*] a paradoxical proposition in that logically that
which is ordained (i.e. *destiny*) cannot be circumvented by wisdom.
68. *ruleth the stars*] governs destiny.
an unlawful means] i.e. the attempted evasion of a sacrifice instituted by
a god.
70–1. *prevent . . . craft*] forestall through my cunning, if possible, the
destiny ordained by the disposition of the stars at your birth.
73. *fearful*] apprehensive.
75–6. *Destiny . . . prevented*] proverbial. Compare *an honourable death is to
be preferred before an infamous life* at lines 80–2 below.
76. *prevented*] forestalled.
77. *drawn to*] compelled into.
80. *over-carefulness*] excessive anxiety.
83. *as*] that.
85. *light*] fall.
86. *fear me*] make me afraid.
87. *Suffer*] Permit.

therefore, to die, for which I was born; or let me curse
that I was born, sith I may not die for it.

Tityrus. Alas, Galatea, to consider the causes of change thou   90
art too young, and that I should find them out for thee,
too too fortunate.

Galatea. The destiny to me cannot be so hard as the disguis-
ing hateful.

Tityrus. To gain love the gods have taken shapes of beasts, and   95
to save life art thou coy to take the attire of men?

Galatea. They were beastly gods, that lust could make them
seem as beasts.

Tityrus. In health it is easy to counsel the sick, but it's hard
for the sick to follow wholesome counsel. Well, let us   100
depart. [*They rise.*] The day is far spent.   *Exeunt.*

1.2.   [*Enter*] CUPID [*and a*] NYMPH *of Diana.*

Cupid. Fair nymph, are you strayed from your company by
chance, or love you to wander solitarily on purpose?

Nymph. Fair boy, or god, or whatever you be, I would you
knew these woods are to me so well known that I cannot
stray though I would, and my mind so free that to be   5
melancholy I have no cause. There is none of Diana's

---

88. *for which . . . born*] as my mortal condition requires (another proverbial expression; see lines 75–6n. above).

89. *sith*] since.

91–2. *that I . . . fortunate*] extremely fortunate that I should be able to
discern them on your behalf.

95. *To gain . . . beasts*] A number of classical myths turn on a god's
assumption of an animal disguise as a means of achieving an amatory goal
(cf. 2.2.21–6 below). Jupiter, for example, took the form of a swan to enjoy
Leda, and mated with Europa in the form of a bull.

96. *coy*] too scrupulous, reluctant.

99. *In health . . . counsel*] a further instance of both speakers' reliance on
proverbial expressions (possibly designed as an index of their naivety).

100. *wholesome counsel*] beneficial advice.

1. *are you strayed*] have you wandered.

2. *solitarily*] on your own.

5. *stray though I would*] get lost even if I wished to.

6. *melancholy*] The desire to be alone was commonly regarded as a
symptom of melancholy in the sixteenth century.

train that any can train, either out of their way or out of
their wits.

Cupid. What is that Diana, a goddess? What her nymphs,
virgins? What her pastimes, hunting? 10

Nymph. A goddess? Who knows it not? Virgins? Who thinks it
not? Hunting? Who loves it not?

Cupid. I pray thee, sweet wench, amongst all your sweet troop
is there not one that followeth the sweetest thing, sweet
love? 15

Nymph. Love, good sir? What mean you by it? Or what do
you call it?

Cupid. A heat full of coldness, a sweet full of bitterness, a pain
full of pleasantness, which maketh thoughts have eyes,
and hearts ears. Bred by desire, nursed by delight, weaned 20
by jealousy, killed by dissembling, buried by ingratitude.
And this is love. Fair lady, will you any?

Nymph. If it be nothing else, it is but a foolish thing.

Cupid. Try, and you shall find it a pretty thing.

Nymph. I have neither will nor leisure, but I will follow Diana 25
in the chase, whose virgins are all chaste, delighting in
the bow that wounds the swift hart in the forest, not
fearing the bow that strikes the soft heart in the chamber.
This difference is between my mistress, Diana, and your
mother, as I guess, Venus, that all her nymphs are amiable 30

---

7. *train / train*] followers / lead astray.

19–20. *maketh thoughts . . . ears*] preternaturally sharpens the communication between the mind, the senses, and the emotions.

20–1. *Bred . . . ingratitude*] The summary charts the successive phases of
an unhappy experience of love.

22. *will you any*] would you like to try it.

24. *pretty*] pleasing.

25. *will nor leisure*] the desire or the time.

26. *chase*] hunt.

27. *bow*] traditionally associated with Diana, goddess of the hunt.

hart] male deer of five or more years.

28. *bow*] the weapon with which Cupid traditionally wounds the hearts
of lovers.

chamber] private room.

30. *her*] Diana's.

amiable] beautiful.

and wise in their kind, the other amorous and too kind
for their sex. And so farewell, little god.   *Exit.*
Cupid. Diana, and thou, and all thine, shall know that Cupid
is a great god. I will practise a while in these woods, and
play such pranks with these nymphs that, while they aim   35
to hit others with their arrows, they shall be wounded
themselves with their own eyes.   *Exit.*

I.3.   [*Enter*] MELIBEUS [*and*] PHILLIDA.

Melibeus. Come, Phillida, fair Phillida, and I fear me too fair,
being my Phillida. Thou knowest the custom of this
country, and I the greatness of thy beauty; we both the
fierceness of the monster, Agar. Everyone thinketh his
own child fair, but I know that which I most desire and   5
would least have, that thou art fairest. Thou shalt therefore disguise thyself in attire, lest I should disguise myself
in affection, in suffering thee to perish by a fond desire,
whom I may preserve by a sure deceit.
Phillida. Dear father, Nature could not make me so fair as she   10
hath made you kind, nor you more kind than me dutiful.
Whatsoever you command I will not refuse, because you
command nothing but my safety and your happiness. But
how shall I be disguised?
Melibeus. In man's apparel.   15

---

31. *in their kind*] by nature.
the other] the followers of Venus.
too kind] too liberal in affection.
34. *practise*] engage in some trickery.
a while] for a time (with a pun on 'wile', a scheme or trick).
36–7. *wounded . . . eyes*] The belief that love was visual in its origins was
widely held in the sixteenth century. Compare *The Merchant of Venice*: 'Tell
me where is Fancy bred? . . . It is engend'red in the eyes, / With gazing fed'
(3.2.63–8).

2. *my Phillida*] i.e. a person of particular value to me.
7. *disguise . . . attire*] conceal your identity by a change of clothes.
7–8. *disguise . . . affection*] act in a way contrary to my natural feelings.
8. *fond desire*] foolish wish (to be father of the fairest).
9. *sure deceit*] infallible deception.
11. *kind*] ready to fulfil your obligations as a parent.

Phillida. It will neither become my body nor my mind.

Melibeus. Why, Phillida?

Phillida. For then I must keep company with boys, and
    commit follies unseemly for my sex, or keep company
    with girls, and be thought more wanton than becometh   20
    me. Besides, I shall be ashamed of my long hose and short
    coat, and so unwarily blab out something by blushing at
    everything.

Melibeus. Fear not, Phillida. Use will make it easy; fear must
    make it necessary.   25

Phillida. I agree, since my father will have it so, and fortune
    must.

Melibeus. Come, let us in, and when thou art disguised, roam
    about these woods till the time be past, and Neptune
    pleased.   *Exeunt.*   30

1.4.   [*Enter*] MARINER, RAFE, ROBIN, *and* DICK
                    [*shipwrecked*].

Robin. Now, Mariner, what callest thou this sport on the sea?

Mariner. It is called a wrack.

Rafe. I take no pleasure in it. Of all deaths, I would not be
    drowned. One's clothes will be so wet when he is taken
    up.   5

Dick. What callest thou the thing we were bound to?

Mariner. A rafter.

---

16. *neither become*] suit neither.

19. *unseemly*] inappropriate.

20. *wanton*] unrestrained in behaviour.

21–2. *long . . . coat*] i.e. typical Elizabethan male attire (doublet and hose).

22. *blab out*] reveal (*blab* literally = blurt).

28. *in*] go in.

2. *wrack*] shipwreck.

4–5. *taken up*] retrieved from the sea.

6. *What . . . bound to*] The question echoes the play on *bound* at 1.1.56–7,
linking the experience of the boys faced by the power of the sea with the
predicaments of the maidens threatened by the wrath of Neptune.

7. *rafter*] spar.

Rafe. I will rather hang myself on a rafter in the house than
be so haled in the sea. There one may have a leap for his
life. But I marvel how our master speeds.   10

Dick. I'll warrant by this time he is wet-shod. Did you
ever see water bubble as the sea did? But what shall
we do?

Mariner. You are now in Lincolnshire, where you can want no
fowl, if you can devise means to catch them. There be   15
woods hard by, and at every mile's end, houses; so that
if you seek on the land, you shall speed better than on
the sea.

Robin. Sea? Nay, I will never sail more. I brook not their diet.
Their bread is so hard that one must carry a whetstone   20
in his mouth to grind his teeth; the meat so salt that one
should think after dinner his tongue had been powdered
ten days.

Rafe. Oh, thou hast a sweet life, Mariner, to be pinned in a
few boards, and to be within an inch of a thing bottom-   25
less. I pray thee, how often hast thou been drowned?

Mariner. Fool, thou seest I am yet alive.

Robin. Why, be they dead that be drowned? I had thought they
had been with the fish, and so by chance been caught up

---

8. *rafter*] beam.
9. *haled*] pulled along.
9–10. *have a leap for his life*] have some control over one's own fate.
10. *marvel . . . speeds*] wonder how the captain of our vessel is faring.
11. *wet-shod*] has water in his shoes (i.e. has wet feet).
14. *Lincolnshire*] county lying to the south of the Humber estuary.
want] lack.
15. *fowl*] birds.
16. *hard by*] close at hand.
at every . . . houses] habitations within a mile of one another.
17. *speed better*] have more success.
19. *brook not*] cannot abide.
20. *whetstone*] shaped stone used for grinding tools (here to sharpen the teeth).
22. *powdered*] salted. Salt was used during this period as a preservative, particularly for the curing of meat.
24. *pinned*] confined.
25. *boards*] planks.
25–6. *to be within . . . bottomless*] to have only an inch (of planking) between you and the sea's endless depths.

with them in a net again. It were a shame a little cold   30
water should kill a man of reason, when you shall see a
poor minnow lie in it that hath no understanding.

Mariner. Thou art wise from the crown of thy head upwards.
Seek you new fortunes now; I will follow mine old. I can
shift the moon and the sun, and know by one card what   35
all you cannot do by a whole pair. The lodestone that
always holdeth his nose to the north, the two-and-thirty
points for the wind, the wonders I see would make all
you blind. You be but boys. I fear the sea no more than
a dish of water. Why, fools, it is but a liquid element.   40
Farewell.   [*He makes as if to go.*]

Robin. [*To his brothers*] It were as good we learned his cunning
at the cards, for we must live by cozenage. We have neither
lands, nor wit, nor masters, nor honesty.

Rafe. Nay, I would have his thirty-two – that is, his three   45
dozen less four – points; for you see betwixt us three there
is not two good points.

---

31. *man of reason*] rational human being.

32. *understanding*] capacity for thought.

33. *wise . . . upwards*] i.e. a fool (the crown being the top of the head).

34–40. *I can . . . element*] The extravagance of the Mariner's claims here
looks forward to the pretentions of Rafe's subsequent masters, the Alchemist
and the Astronomer, in 2.3 and 3.3, who assert a similar god-like power. See
Introduction, p. 8.

35. *shift*] a nautical term signifying 'to record the variations in the position
of' (the dominant meaning here) but also capable of being interpreted as 'to
exchange the places of' or 'move'.

card] mariner's card, a circular piece of stiff paper on which the thirty-two
points of the compass are marked.

36. *whole pair*] an entire pack (with a pun on *card* = mariner's compass
card / playing card).

36–7. *lodestone . . . north*] magnet which always points to the north.

37–8. *two-and-thirty points*] thirty-two points of the compass by which the
direction of the wind may be determined. The term 'point' also signified the
tagged lace used for fastening hose, hence Rafe's confusion at lines 45ff.

39–40. *I fear . . . element*] Compare the mastery over the elements (earth,
air, fire, and water, of which all matter was thought to be composed) claimed
by Rafe's subsequent masters in 2.3 and 3.3.

43. *cards*] playing cards, to which Robin believes the Mariner's use of the
word refers.

we must . . . cozenage] See Characters in Order of Appearance, lines 7, 8,
9n. for the boys' propensity to live by their wits. *cozenage* = cheating.

46. *points*] See lines 37–8n. above.

Dick. Let us call him a little back that we may learn those points. [*To the Mariner*] Sirrah, a word. I pray thee, show us thy points. 50

Mariner. [*Returning*] Will you learn?

Dick. Ay.

Mariner. Then as you like this, I will instruct you in all our secrets; for there is not a clout, nor card, nor board, nor post, that hath not a special name or singular 55 nature.

Dick. Well, begin with your points, for I lack only points in this world.

Mariner. North. North and by east. North northeast. North-east and by north. Northeast. Northeast and by east. East 60 northeast. East and by north. East.

Dick. I'll say it. North. Northeast. Northeast. Nore nore and by nore-east. I shall never do it!

Mariner. This is but one quarter.

Robin. I shall never learn a quarter of it. I will try. North. 65 Northeast is by the west side. North and by north.

Dick. Passing ill.

Mariner. Hast thou no memory? [*To Rafe*] Try thou.

Rafe. North. North and by north – I can go no further.

Mariner. O dullard! Is thy head lighter than the wind and 70 thy tongue so heavy it will not wag? I will once again say it.

---

49. *Sirrah*] a term of address used towards a social inferior, and thus ludicrously inappropriate here.

54. *clout*] piece of cloth.

card] See line 35n. above.

55. *singular*] particular.

59–72.] The exchange parodies the rote learning of foreign languages (particularly Latin) in sixteenth-century schools, with the Mariner in the role of exasperated master and the boys as slow-witted schoolboys.

62. *Nore*] variant of 'nor', i.e. north.

64. *quarter*] quadrant, one of the four segments of the compass, running in this instance from north to east.

67. *Passing ill*] exceptionally bad.

70. *dullard*] dunce.

71. *wag*] move.

Rafe. I will never learn this language. It will get but small
     living, when it will scarce be learned till one be old.
Mariner. Nay then, farewell. And if your fortunes exceed not   75
     your wits, you shall starve before ye sleep.   [*Exit.*]
Rafe. Was there ever such cozening? Come, let us to the woods
     and see what fortunes we may have before they be made
     ships. As for our master, he is drowned.
Dick. I will this way.   80
Robin. I this.
Rafe. I this; and this day twelvemonth let us all meet here
     again. It may be we shall either beg together or hang
     together.
Dick. It skills not, so we be together. But let us sing now,   85
     though we cry hereafter.   [*They sing.*]

Omnes.   Rocks, shelves, and sands and seas, farewell.
                  Fie! Who would dwell
                  In such a hell
             As is a ship, which drunk does reel,   90
             Taking salt healths from deck to keel?

Robin.   Up were we swallowed in wet graves,
Dick.   All soused in waves,

73–4. *get . . . living*] bring little to live on.

74. *scarce*] hardly.

75–6. *exceed . . . wits*] are not greater than your intelligence.

77. *such cozening*] cheating comparable with this.

78–9. *before . . . ships*] The ironic comment probably refers to the deple-
tion of English woods as a consequence of the extensive ship-building pro-
gramme initiated by Elizabeth I in 1584.

80. *I . . . way*] I will go in this direction.

82. *this day twelvemonth*] on this date in twelve month's time.

85. *skills not*] doesn't matter.

87–105.] In common with the majority of songs in the Lylian corpus, the
sung material was not included in the play when first published but was
restored to the work in the first collected edition of the dramatist's plays
published by Edward Blount in 1632.

87. Omnes] All.

shelves] sandbanks.

90. *drunk*] lurching as if intoxicated.

91. *Taking salt healths*] Taking in salt water.

93. *soused*] drenched.

Rafe.	By Neptune's slaves.	
Omnes.	What shall we do, being tossed to shore?	95
Robin.	Milk some blind tavern, and there roar.	

Rafe.	'Tis brave, my boys, to sail on land,	
	For being well manned	
	We can cry, 'Stand!'	
Dick.	The trade of pursing ne'er shall fail,	100
	Until the hangman cries, 'Strike sail!'	

Omnes.	Rove, then, no matter whither,	
	In fair and stormy weather,	
	And as we live, let's die together.	
	One hempen caper cuts a feather.	105

Exeunt [in different directions].

---

94. *Neptune's slaves*] The instruments of the god of the sea (i.e. wind and water, recalling the violence of the coming of the Agar).

96. *Milk . . . tavern*] Cheat in some unsuspecting tavern.

roar] revel without restraint.

97. *brave*] splendid.

98–9. *For being . . . 'Stand'*] There being a number of us, we are in a position to take purses on the highway (with a reference to the highwayman's cry of 'Stand and deliver'). The terms *well manned* and *Stand* also carry the bawdy implication that the boys are virile (*well manned*) and capable of having an erection (*Stand*).

100. *pursing*] taking purses.

101. *'Strike sail'*] nautical command to lower the sails at the close of a voyage (here the journey of life, terminated by the hangman) or to concede defeat.

102. *Rove*] Roam.

105. *hempen caper*] dance at the end of a rope.

cuts a feather] a proverbial expression signifying to make a fine or subtle distinction (here the division effected by the jerk of a rope between life and death). The expression is particularly appropriate in this context in that it was also used of water foaming before the bow of a ship.

Act 2

[Enter] GALATEA *alone.*

Galatea. Blush, Galatea, that must frame thy affection fit for
thy habit, and therefore be thought immodest because
thou art unfortunate. Thy tender years cannot dissemble
this deceit, nor thy sex bear it. Oh, would the gods had
made me as I seem to be, or that I may safely be what I   5
seem not! Thy father doteth, Galatea, whose blind love
corrupteth his fond judgement, and, jealous of thy death,
seemeth to dote on thy beauty; whose fond care carrieth
his partial eye as far from truth as his heart is from false-
hood. But why dost thou blame him, or blab what thou   10
art, when thou shouldst only counterfeit what thou art
not? But whist, here cometh a lad. I will learn of him how
to behave myself.

            Enter PHILLIDA *in man's attire.*

Phillida. *[To herself]* I neither like my gait nor my garments,
the one untoward, the other unfit, both unseemly. Oh,   15

1–2. *frame . . . habit*] adapt your preferences to suit your attire.
3–4. *dissemble this deceit*] sustain (through dissembling) this deception.
5. *as I . . . be*] i.e. a boy.
5–6. *what . . . not*] i.e. girl.
6. *doteth*] (*a*) loves you to excess; (*b*) is mad (cf. the play on *fond* in lines
7 and 8 below).
7. *fond*] (*a*) loving; (*b*) foolish. The word is repeated with the same double
meaning in the following line.
jealous] fearful.
9. *partial eye*] vision distorted by his own affection.
10. *blab*] betray (through speech).
11. *only counterfeit*] merely pretend to be.
12. *whist*] hush.
13. *behave*] conduct.
14. *my gait*] the way I walk (indicating Phillida has adopted a boyish stride).
15. *untoward*] awkward.
unfit] unsuitable for one of my sex.
unseemly] improper.

Phillida! [*She sees Galatea.*] But yonder stayeth one, and
therefore say nothing, but 'Oh, Phillida!'

Galatea. [*Aside*] I perceive that boys are in as great disliking
of themselves as maids. Therefore, though I wear the
apparel, I am glad I am not the person.   20

Phillida. [*Aside*] It is a pretty boy and a fair. He might well
have been a woman; but because he is not, I am glad I
am. For now, under the colour of my coat, I shall decipher
the follies of their kind.

Galatea. [*Aside*] I would salute him, but I fear I should make   25
a curtsy instead of a leg.

Phillida. [*Aside*] If I durst trust my face as well as I do my
habit, I would spend some time to make pastime; for say
what they will of a man's wit, it is no second thing to be
a woman.   30

Galatea. [*Aside*] All the blood in my body would be in my
face if he should ask me, as the question among men is
common, 'Are you a maid?'

Phillida. [*Aside*] But why stand I still? Boys should be bold.
But here cometh a brave train that will spill all our talk.   35

Enter DIANA, TELUSA, *and* EUROTA.

Diana. God speed, fair boy.

Galatea. You are deceived, lady.

---

16. *stayeth one*] someone is standing.

22–3. *because he . . . am*] Though justified in the following lines by the
desire to gain an insight into male behaviour, the comment hints at the
instant attraction between the disguised maidens, in that Phillida is glad that
the seeming youth is not a woman, like herself.

23. *colour . . . coat*] false appearance afforded by my clothes. *colour* = 'cloak'
or 'guise' here, rather than 'hue', while *coat* is a generic term for 'dress'.

decipher] detect.

24. *kind*] sex.

25. *salute*] greet.

26. *leg*] bow, executed with one leg drawn back and the other bent.

28. *habit*] clothes.

make pastime] have some amusement.

29–30. *no second . . . woman*] a woman is by no means inferior.

33. *maid*] virgin.

35. *brave train*] fine-looking troop of people.

spill] ruin.

36. *God speed*] May God prosper you (a conventional salutation).

Diana. Why, are you no boy?

Galatea. No fair boy.

Diana. But, I see, an unhappy boy.   40

Telusa. Saw you not the deer come this way? He flew down
the wind, and I believe you have blanched him.

Galatea. Whose dear was it, lady?

Telusa. Diana's deer.

Galatea. I saw none but mine own dear.   45

Telusa. This wag is wanton, or a fool. Ask the other, Diana.

Galatea. [*Aside*] I know not how it cometh to pass, but yonder
boy is in mine eye too beautiful. I pray gods the ladies
think him not their dear.

Diana. [*To Phillida*] Pretty lad, do your sheep feed in the   50
forest, or are you strayed from your flock, or on purpose
come ye to mar Diana's pastime?

Phillida. I understand not one word that you speak.

Diana. What, art thou neither lad nor shepherd?

Phillida. My mother said I could be no lad till I was twenty   55
year old, nor keep sheep till I could tell them. And therefore, lady, neither lad nor shepherd is here.

Telusa. These boys are both agreed; either they are very pleasant, or too perverse. You were best, lady, make them tusk

---

39. *No fair boy*] By seemingly disputing that she is *fair*, Galatea recovers
her error in instinctively rejecting Diana's greeting.

41. *deer*] The differentiation between the homophones 'deer' and 'dear' in
modern spelling obscures the misunderstandings generated in speech in the
course of the subsequent exchange.

41–2. *flew ... wind*] sped away in the same direction as the wind (to
prevent the hunters following his scent).

42. *blanched him*] caused him to turn back.

45. *I saw ... dear*] The response is indicative that Galatea is already
attracted to Phillida, whom she presumes to be a youth (cf. Phillida's
comment at lines 22–3 above).

46. *wag*] mischievous boy.

wanton] overly high-spirited.

47–9. *I know ... dear*] The comment reveals that Galatea has still failed to
grasp the nature of the pursuit in which Diana and her nymphs are engaged.

52. *mar Diana's pastime*] ruin the pleasures of the goddess of the hunt.

54, 55. *lad / lad*] youth / term used in pastoral poetry for a shepherd boy.

56. *tell*] count.

58. *agreed*] alike.

58–9. *pleasant*] facetious, merry.

59. *perverse*] awkward, disobliging.

tusk] beat (to startle the game).

these woods whilst we stand with our bows, and so use   60
them as beagles, since they have such good mouths.

Diana. I will. [*To Phillida*] Follow me without delay or excuse,
and if you can do nothing, yet shall you halloo the deer.

Phillida. I am willing to go. [*Aside*] Not for these ladies'
company, because myself am a virgin, but for that fair   65
boy's favour, who I think be a god.

Diana. [*To Galatea*] You, sir boy, shall also go.

Galatea. I must, if you command. [*Aside*] And would, if you
had not.   *Exeunt.*

2.2.   [*Enter*] CUPID *alone, in nymph's apparel,*
                              and NEPTUNE *listening.*

Cupid. Now, Cupid, under the shape of a silly girl show the
power of a mighty god. Let Diana and all her coy nymphs
know that there is no heart so chaste but thy bow can
wound, nor eyes so modest but thy brands can kindle,
nor thoughts so stayed but thy shafts can make wavering,   5
weak, and wanton. Cupid, though he be a child, is no
baby. I will make their pains my pastimes, and so
confound their loves in their own sex that they shall dote

---

61. *beagles*] breed of dog used in hunting.

good mouths] readiness to bark (i.e. talk).

63. *halloo*] startle by shouting.

65. *because . . . virgin*] in that I am a member of the same sex.

65–6. *for that . . . favour*] (*a*) because of that handsome boy's looks; (*b*) to
gain that handsome boy's regard.

1. *silly*] simple, helpless (also at line 18 below).

2. *coy*] disdainful.

4. *brands*] firebrands, the burning torches traditionally carried by Cupid
to ignite the flames of love.

5. *stayed*] steadfast.

shafts] arrows, the traditional means by which Cupid wounded lovers'
hearts.

6. *wanton*] unruly.

7. *pastimes*] pleasures.

8. *confound . . . sex*] throw their desires into confusion by directing them
to those of their own sex.

dote] be mad (with a pun on 'dote' i.e. to love to excess).

in their desires, delight in their affections, and practise
only impossibilities. Whilst I truant from my mother,   10
I will use some tyranny in these woods, and so shall
their exercise in foolish love be my excuse for running
away. I will see whether fair faces be always chaste, or
Diana's virgins only modest, else will I spend both my
shafts and shifts. And then, ladies, if you see these dainty   15
dames entrapped in love, say softly to yourselves, 'We
may all love'.   *Exit.*
Neptune. [*Coming forward*] Do silly shepherds go about to
deceive great Neptune in putting on man's attire upon
women? And Cupid, to make sport, deceive them all by   20
using a woman's apparel upon a god? Then, Neptune,
that hast taken sundry shapes to obtain love, stick not to
practise some deceit to show thy deity; and having often
thrust thyself into the shape of beasts to deceive men, be
not coy to use the shape of a shepherd to show thyself a   25
god. Neptune cannot be overreached by swains, himself

---

9. *affections*] passions.

9–10. *practise only impossibilities*] pursue nothing but that which cannot be
achieved.

10. *my mother*] Venus, goddess of love.

11. *use*] practise.

11–13. *so shall . . . away*] in this way, causing Diana's nymphs to fall in
love will justify my running away (in the eyes of Diana's rival, Venus).

14. *only*] uniquely, pre-eminently.

14–15. *else . . . shifts*] or I will exhaust (*spend*) both my arrows and my
devices (*shifts*).

15. *And then, ladies*] The direct address to the female members of the
audience serves to draw the spectators into the events taking place in the
play world, and to suggest their relevance to them.

22. *that hast . . love*] The classical deities frequently adopted animal forms
in order to fulfil their amatory desires (cf. 1.1.95n.). Neptune became a horse,
for example, to pursue Ceres, and a ram to win Theophane, by whom he
became the father of the ram with the golden fleece. Oddly, the disguise
adopted here by Neptune plays no part in subsequent events.

sundry] various.

stick not] do not scruple.

24–5. *be not coy*] do not be reluctant.

25. *use*] adopt.

26. *overreached by swains*] deceived by country folk.

is subtle, and if Diana be overtaken by craft, Cupid is
wise. I will into these woods and mark all, and in the end
will mar all.   *Exit.*

2.3.   *Enter* RAFE *alone.*

Rafe. Call you this seeking of fortunes, when one can find
   nothing but birds' nests? Would I were out of these
   woods, for I shall have but wooden luck. Here's nothing
   but the screaking of owls, croaking of frogs, hissing
   of adders, barking of foxes, walking of hags. But what   5
   be these?

         Enter FAIRIES, *dancing and playing, and so exeunt.*

   I will follow them. To hell I shall not go, for so fair faces
   never can have such hard fortunes. What black boy is this?

27–8. *if Diana . . . wise*] an ironic observation implying that just as
Neptune is too wise to be deceived by shepherds, so Diana is too shrewd to
be outwitted by Cupid.

28. *mark all*] observe everything that happens.

29. *mar*] ruin.

2. *Would I*] I wish I.

3. *wooden*] paltry. The term is used in opposition to one denoting a high
value material (e.g. golden) and sustains the pun on *would* initiated in the
previous line.

4. *screaking*] uttering a shrill harsh cry (cf. screech-owl, an alternative
name for the barn owl).

owls] birds of ill omen.

5. *hags*] evil spirits in female form said to haunt trees and bushes by night.

6.1. *FAIRIES*] constructed as potentially malign in the sixteenth century,
rather than as the delicate beings of children's fiction.

7. *so*] such.

8. *hard*] ugly, foul. Compare the similar opposition between fair faces
and hard fortunes at 2.4.9–10.

black boy] The stage spectacle here turns upon false appearance. The *fair
faces* of the Fairies may conceal a malign nature and lure Rafe into the flames
of hell, while the seemingly diabolic *black boy* is, in fact, a harmless apprentice, obliged to labour over a much less terrible fire.

Enter the Alchemist's boy, PETER *[covered in soot].*

Peter. [*To himself*] What a life do I lead with my master!
  Nothing but blowing of bellows, beating of spirits, and   10
  scraping of crosslets. It is a very secret science, for none
  almost can understand the language of it: sublimation,
  almigation, calcination, rubification, incorporation, circination, cementation, albification, and fermentation, with
  as many terms unpossible to be uttered as the art to be   15
  compassed.
Rafe. [*Aside*] Let me cross myself! I never heard so many
  devils in a little monkey's mouth!
Peter. Then our instruments: crosslets, sublivatories, cucurbits, limbecks, descensories, vials manual and mural for   20

9–28.] The seemingly unholy gibberish uttered by Peter here functions as
an aural contrast to the harmonious 'playing' of the Fairies (cf. the visual
oppositions discussed in the previous note), confirming Rafe's belief that the
black boy is a fiend. The alchemical terms appear to have been largely derived
by Lyly from Chaucer's 'Canon's Yeoman's Tale' in *The Canterbury Tales*.

10. *spirits*] the four liquid essences defined by medieval alchemists.

11. *crosslets*] crucibles.

11–12. *It is . . . of it*] Compare the special language of the Mariner's profession at 1.4.53ff. above and the obscure terms of the Astronomer's art at
3.3.38ff.

12. *sublimation*] turning a solid substance into a vapour which then re-
solidifies when cool.

13. *almigation*] amalgamation (the softening of a metal through combining with mercury).
calcination] reduction (through the application of heat) to powder form.
rubification] the process of heating a substance until it turns red.
incorporation] the combining of substances to form a homogenous
compound.

13–14. *circination*] revolving.

14. *cementation*] combining one substance with another at high tempera-
ture without liquefaction.
albification] whitening.

16. *compassed*] mastered.

17. *cross myself*] make the sign of the cross (to ward off evil spirits).

18. *little monkey's*] mischievous boy's (with diabolic overtones, in that
devils were frequently depicted as monkeys or apes).

19. *crosslets*] See line 11n. above.
sublivatories] vessels used in sublimation (see line 12n. above).

19–20. *cucurbits*] vessels used in distillation.

20. *limbecks*] chemical retorts used for distillation.
descensories] apparatus used for distilling downwards (i.e. with heat applied
at the top of the vessel).

imbibing and conbibing, bellows mollificative and
indurative.

Rafe. [*Aside*] What language is this? Do they speak so?

Peter. Then our metals: saltpetre, vitriol, sal tartar, sal preparate, argol, resagar, sal ammoniac, agrimony, lumany,   25
brimstone, valerian, tartar alum, breemwort, glass,
unslaked lime, chalk, ashes, hair, and what not, to make
I know not what.

Rafe. [*Aside*] My hair beginneth to stand upright! Would the
boy would make an end!   30

Peter. And yet such a beggarly science it is, and so strong on
multiplication, that the end is to have neither gold, wit,
nor honesty.

Rafe. [*Coming forward*] Then am I just of your occupation.
What, fellow, well met!   35

20–1. *vials . . . conbibing*] hand-held and wall-mounted vessels for mois-
tening and mixing.

21–2. *mollificative and indurative*] for softening and hardening.

23. *they*] devils. Rafe continues to believe that the boy is a fiend talking
in a diabolic language.

24. *saltpetre*] potassium nitrate, the chief ingredient of gunpowder.

vitriol] sulphuric acid, or any of its salts.

sal tartar] salt of tartar (bitartrate of potash).

24–5. *sal preparate*] prepared salt.

25. *argol*] crude bitartrate of potassium.

resager] realgar (disulphide of arsenic, a red powder used as a pigment
and in pyrotechnics).

sal ammoniac] ammonium chloride.

agrimony] genus of plant with small yellow flowers.

lumany] unknown. The term may be a compositorial error for 'lunary' (a
plant used in relation to charms), or with reference to silver (referred to by
alchemists as 'lunar'). The likelihood that the former is intended here is
supported by the reference to the plant at 3.1.22 below.

26. *brimstone*] sulphur.

valerian] strong-smelling herb with pink or white flowers.

tartar alum] separate terms for distinct substances, used here (erroneously)
for a single compound. *tartar* = bitartrate of potash / *alum* = a double sulphate
of aluminium and potassium. The error is repeated at lines 103–4 below.

breemwort] barm, yeast.

27. *unslaked lime*] lime unmixed with water.

32. *multiplication*] augmenting precious metals through the transmutation
of baser ones.

34. *occupation*] profession (in this case, that of feckless youth in search of
a living).

35. *fellow*] comrade.

Peter. Fellow? Upon what acquaintance?

Rafe. Why, thou sayst the end of thy occupation is to have
neither wit, money, nor honesty; and methinks, at a blush,
thou shouldst be one of my occupation.

Peter. Thou art deceived. My master is an alchemist.   40

Rafe. What's that? A man?

Peter. A little more than a man, and a hair's breadth less than
a god. He can make of thy cap, gold, and by multiplication of one groat, three old angels. I have known him of
the tag of a point to make a silver bowl of a pint.   45

Rafe. That makes thee have never a point; they be all turned
to pots. But if he can do this, he shall be a god
altogether.

Peter. If thou have any gold to work on, thou art then made
for ever. For with one pound of gold, he will go near to   50
pave ten acres of ground.

Rafe. How might a man serve him, and learn his cunning?

Peter. Easily. First seem to understand the terms, and
specially mark these points. In our art there are four
spirits.   55

Rafe. Nay, I have done, if you work with devils.

---

38. *at a blush*] at first glance.

43. *make . . . gold*] turn your cap into gold.

44. *groat*] silver coin worth fourpence in pre-decimalization English
currency.

angels] gold coins bearing the device of the archangel Michael, each worth
approximately twenty groats. *old angels* (i.e those minted prior to the acces-
sion of Mary Tudor) were highly valued for the purity of the metal from
which they were struck.

45. *tag of a point*] metal tip of the lace used for fastening hose.

of a pint] able to hold a pint.

46. *have . . . point*] lack even one point (to hold up your hose).

50. *go near to*] almost.

52–77.] The following exchange echoes the Mariner's attempt to teach the
shipwrecked boys the terms of his profession (see 1.4.51ff.).

52. *cunning*] art, skill.

55. *spirits*] (*a*) liquid essences (the sense in which Peter understands the
term); (*b*) supernatural beings (the meaning Rafe attributes to him in the
next line).

Peter. Thou art gross. We call those spirits that are the grounds
of our art, and, as it were, the metals more incorporative
for domination. The first spirit is quicksilver.

Rafe. That is my spirit, for my silver is so quick that I   60
have much ado to catch it, and when I have it, it is so
nimble that I cannot hold it. I thought there was a devil
in it.

Peter. The second, orpiment.

Rafe. That's no spirit, but a word to conjure a spirit.   65

Peter. The third, sal ammoniac.

Rafe. A proper word.

Peter. The fourth, brimstone.

Rafe. That's a stinking spirit. I thought there was some spirit
in it because it burned so blue. For my mother would   70
often tell me that when the candle burned blue there was
some ill spirit in the house, and now I perceive it was the
spirit Brimstone.

Peter. Thou canst remember these four spirits?

Rafe. Let me alone to conjure them.   75

Peter. Now are there also seven bodies – but here cometh my
master!

---

57. *gross*] dull-witted.

grounds] foundation.

58–9. *more . . . domination*] more capable of combining for ascendancy or
control over other substances.

59. *quicksilver*] mercury.

60. *That . . . spirit*] Rafe continues to suppose that *spirit* refers to a supernatural entity (here one governing his life) as his responses at lines 65 and
69ff. confirm).

64. *orpiment*] yellow arsenic, trisulphide of arsenic, used as a dye.

65. *conjure*] summon.

66. *sal ammoniac*] ammonium chloride.

68. *brimstone*] sulphur.

69–70. *That's . . . blue*] The comment turns on the fact that brimstone
smells unpleasant and burns with a blue flame.

76. *seven bodies*] the seven metals known to the ancient world (gold,
silver, mercury, copper, iron, tin, and lead). Anne Lancashire notes in
her Regents Renaissance Drama series edition of the play (Lincolon,
NE. 1969) that the philosopher's stone (capable of transmuting base metals
into gold) was reputedly compounded of the seven bodies and the four
spirits.

Enter [the] ALCHEMIST *[lost in thought].*

Rafe. This is a beggar.

Peter. No, such cunning men must disguise themselves as
though there were nothing in them, for otherwise they   80
shall be compelled to work for princes, and so be constrained to bewray their secrets.

Rafe. I like not his attire, but am enamoured of his art.

Alchemist. [*To himself*] An ounce of silver, limed, as much of
crude mercury, of spirits four, being tempered with the   85
bodies seven, by multiplying of it ten times, comes for
one pound, eight thousand pounds, so that I may have
only beechen coals.

Rafe. [*To Peter*] Is it possible?

Peter. It is more than certainty.   90

Rafe. I'll tell thee one secret. I stole a silver thimble. Dost
thou think that he will make it a pottle pot?

Peter. A pottle pot? Nay, I dare warrant it, a whole cupboard
of plate! Why, of the quintessence of a leaden plummet
he hath framed twenty dozen of silver spoons. Look how   95
he studies. I durst venture my life he is now casting about
how of his breath he may make golden bracelets, for
oftentimes of smoke he hath made silver drops.

Rafe. [*In amazement*] What do I hear?

---

79. *cunning*] wise, learned.

80. *there . . . them*] they had no special knowledge.

82. *bewray*] reveal.

84. *limed*] obscure. Possibly 'steeped in a solution of lime and water' or a
misreading of Chaucer's 'silver lemaille', i.e. silver filings.

86–7. *for . . . pounds*] to eight thousand pounds from one pound.

87. *so that*] if only.

88. *beechen coals*] beech-wood firing, highly prized by alchemists for the
speed and intensity with which it burns.

92. *pottle pot*] a half-gallon (i.e. four pint) container (frequently applied
to a drinking vessel).

94. *plate*] silverware.

quintessence] five times refined essence.

95. *framed*] made.

96. *casting about*] considering.

98. *drops*] ear-rings or pendants.

Peter. Didst thou never hear how Jupiter came in a golden   100
    shower to Danae?

Rafe. I remember that tale.

Peter. That shower did my master make of a spoonful of tartar
    alum. But with the fire of blood and the corrosive of the
    air, he is able to make nothing infinite. – But whist, he   105
    espieth us.

Alchemist. [*To Peter*] What, Peter, do you loiter, knowing that
    every minute increaseth our mine?

Peter. I was glad to take the air, for the metal came so fast
    that I feared my face would have been turned to silver.   110

Alchemist. [*Noticing Rafe*] But what stripling is this?

Peter. One that is desirous to learn your craft.

Alchemist. Craft, sir boy? You must call it a mystery.

Rafe. All is one: a crafty mystery and a mystical craft.

Alchemist. Canst thou take pains?   115

Rafe. Infinite.

Alchemist. But thou must be sworn to be secret, and then I
    will entertain thee.

100–1. *Jupiter . . . Danae*] Unable to gain access to Danae, confined to a
tower by her father, who had been informed by a soothsayer that her child
would cause his death, Jupiter transformed himself into a shower of gold,
becoming the father of Perseus by her.

103–4. *tartar alum*] See line 26n. above.

104–5. *fire . . . air*] obscure. The terms may denote the warmth imparted
by blood and the corroding properties of wind, but no comparable example
has been traced.

105. *nothing infinite*] (*a*) innumerable things from nothing (the sense that
Peter superficially intends); (*b*) an infinite amount of nothing (the reality of
the Alchemist's art).

106. *espieth*] sees.

108. *mine*] hoard.

111. *stripling*] youth.

112. *craft*] occupation requiring particular skills.

113. *mystery*] occupation requiring the mastery of a field of knowledge
(used here with connotations of the arcane).

114. *All is one*] It's the same thing.

115. *take pains*] (*a*) work conscientiously (the sense the Alchemist
intends); (*b*) endure suffering (the sense in which Rafe, from grim experience, understands him).

117. *be sworn*] (*a*) take an oath (the Alchemist's meaning); (*b*) utter an
oath (the sense Rafe humorously attributes to him at lines 119–20).

118. *entertain thee*] admit you into my service.

Rafe. I can swear, though I be a poor fellow, as well as the
    best man in the shire. But, sir, I much marvel that you,   120
    being so cunning, should be so ragged.
Alchemist. Oh, my child, gryphes make their nests of gold,
    though their coats are feathers, and we feather our nests
    with diamonds, though our garments be but frieze. If
    thou knewest the secret of this science, the cunning   125
    would make thee so proud that thou wouldst disdain the
    outward pomp.
Peter. My master is so ravished with his art that we many
    times go supperless to bed, for he will make gold of his
    bread; and such is the drought of his desire that we all   130
    wish our very guts were gold.
Rafe. I have good fortune to light upon such a master.
Alchemist. When in the depth of my skill I determine to try
    the uttermost of mine art, I am dissuaded by the gods.
    Otherwise, I durst undertake to make the fire as it flames,   135
    gold; the wind as it blows, silver; the water as it runs, lead;
    the earth as it stands, iron; the sky, brass; and men's
    thoughts, firm metals.
Rafe. I must bless myself, and marvel at you.
Alchemist. Come in, and thou shalt see all.   *Exit.*   140
Rafe. I follow, I run, I fly! They say my father hath a golden
    thumb; you shall see me have a golden body!   *Exit.*

119-20. *I can . . . shire*] an allusion to the conventional association
between profanity and social position. Compare the proverbial expression
'to swear like a lord'.

120. *much marvel*] wonder a great deal.

121. *being so cunning*] having such knowledge.

122. *gryphes*] griffins, legendary creatures, with the head and wings of an
eagle and the body of a lion.

123. *feather our nests*] enrich ourselves.

124. *frieze*] coarse woollen cloth.

125. *cunning*] knowledge.

130. *drought . . . desire*] extremity of his thirst to achieve his goal.

139. *marvel*] wonder.

141-2. *my father . . . thumb*] a proverbial attribute of millers from their
reputed practise of giving short measure (and thus enriching themselves) by
pressing down the scales with their thumbs when weighing out flour. See
Characters in Order of Appearance, lines 7, 8, 9n.

Peter. I am glad of this, for now I shall have leisure to run
away. Such a bald art as never was! Let him keep his new
man, for he shall never see his old again. God shield me   145
from blowing gold to nothing, with a strong imagination
to make nothing anything!   *Exit.*

2.4.   [*Enter*] GALATEA *alone.*

Galatea. How now, Galatea? Miserable Galatea, that having
put on the apparel of a boy thou canst not also put on
the mind! O fair Melibeus! Ay, too fair, and therefore, I
fear, too proud. Had it not been better for thee to have
been a sacrifice to Neptune than a slave to Cupid; to die   5
for thy country than to live in thy fancy; to be a sacrifice
than a lover? Oh, would when I hunted his eye with my
heart he might have seen my heart with his eyes! Why did
Nature to him, a boy, give a face so fair, or to me, a virgin,
a fortune so hard? I will now use for the distaff the bow,   10
and play at quoits abroad that was wont to sew in my
sampler at home. It may be, Galatea – foolish Galatea,
what may be? Nothing. Let me follow him into the woods,
and thou, sweet Venus, be my guide.   *Exit.*

---

144. *Such . . . was*] There was never such an unproductive trade.

145. *man*] servant.

146. *blowing . . . nothing*] expending money and energy on a process that
yields nothing.

2–3. *put on . . . mind*] assumed the clothing of a boy you cannot think like
one as well.

3. *O fair Melibeus*] The exclamation reveals that the disguised maidens
have adopted their fathers' names. Compare Eurota's reference to Galatea
as 'Tityrus' at 3.1.67.

7. *his*] the disguised Phillida's (rather than Cupid's).

10. *hard*] ugly, foul.

distaff] cleft stick on which flax or wool was wound (used here to denote
those occupations appropriate to a woman).

11. *quoits*] popular men's game, involving throwing hoops at a peg (used
here to signify masculine pastimes).

abroad] out of doors.

12. *sampler*] piece of embroidery designed to exhibit the maker's skill
through the variety of stitches employed.

2.5.   *Enter* PHILLIDA *alone.*

Phillida. Poor Phillida, curse the time of thy birth and rare-
      ness of thy beauty, the unaptness of thy apparel and the
      untamedness of thy affections! Art thou no sooner in the
      habit of a boy but thou must be enamoured of a boy?
      What shalt thou do, when what best liketh thee most   5
      discontenteth thee? Go into the woods, watch the good
      times, his best moods, and transgress in love a little of
      thy modesty. I will! – I dare not. Thou must! – I cannot.
      Then pine in thine own peevishness. I will not! – I will.
      Ah, Phillida, do something, nay, anything, rather than live   10
      thus. Well, what I will do myself knows not, but what I
      ought I know too well. And so I go, resolute either to
      bewray my love, or to suffer shame.   *Exit.*

1–2. *rareness*] exceptional nature.

2. *unaptness*] inappropriateness.

3. *affections*] desires.

4. *habit*] clothing.
enamoured of] in love with.

5–6. *what best . . . discontenteth thee*] the thing that pleases you most (i.e.
the sight of the disguised Galatea) causes you greatest unhappiness.

7–8. *transgress . . . modesty*] exceed the bounds of what you deem to be
modest in the interests of love.

9. *peevishness*] foolishness.

12. *ought*] ought to do (i.e. conquer her feelings).

13. *bewray*] reveal.

Act 3

3.1.   [*Enter*] TELUSA *alone.*

Telusa. How now? What new conceits, what strange contraries,
breed in thy mind? Is thy Diana become a Venus, thy chaste
thoughts turned to wanton looks, thy conquering modesty
to a captive imagination? Beginnest thou, with pyralis, to die
in the air and live in the fire, to leave the sweet delight of   5
hunting, and to follow the hot desire of love? Oh, Telusa,
these words are unfit for thy sex, being a virgin, but apt for
thy affections, being a lover. And can there in years so young,
in education so precise, in vows so holy, and in a heart so
chaste, enter either a strong desire, or a wish, or a wavering   10
thought of love? Can Cupid's brands quench Vesta's flames,
and his feeble shafts headed with feathers pierce deeper than
Diana's arrows headed with steel? Break thy bow, Telusa,
that seekest to break thy vow, and let those hands that aimed
to hit the wild hart scratch out those eyes that have wounded   15
thy tame heart. O vain and only naked name of chastity,

0.1.] The structure of the scene that follows, with its series of entries,
concealments, and parallel admissions of love, is echoed by Shakespeare in
4.3 of *Love's Labour's Lost.*

1. *conceits*] notions.

strange contraries] See Cupid's description of the paradoxical nature of love
at 1.2.18–21.

2. *Is thy . . . Venus*] have you exchanged Love for Chastity as your goddess.

4. *captive imagination*] enthralled state of mind.

pyralis] winged insect thought to live in fire and die when removed from
it (proverbial for the fleeting nature of happiness).

9. *in education so precise*] so scrupulously brought up.

11. *Cupid's brands*] See 2.2.4n.

Vesta's flames] the eternal fire, tended by virgin priestesses (the Vestal
Virgins), burning in the temple of Vesta, chaste goddess of the hearth.

12. *shafts*] arrows.

15. *hart*] male deer after its fifth year.

16. *only naked name of*] merely empty term.

that is made eternal, and perisheth by time; holy, and is
infected by fancy; divine, and is made mortal by folly!
Virgins' hearts, I perceive, are not unlike cotton trees, whose
fruit is so hard in the bud it soundeth like steel, and, being   20
ripe, poureth forth nothing but wool; and their thoughts like
the leaves of lunary, which the further they grow from the
sun, the sooner they are scorched with his beams. Oh,
Melibeus, because thou art fair must I be fickle, and false
my vow because I see thy virtue? Fond girl that I am, to   25
think of love; nay, vain profession that I follow, to disdain
love! But here cometh Eurota. I must now put on a red
mask and blush, lest she perceive my pale face and laugh.

Enter EUROTA.

Eurota. Telusa, Diana bid me hunt you out, and saith that you
care not to hunt with her; but if you follow any other   30
game than she hath roused, your punishment shall be to
bend all our bows and weave all our strings. Why look ye
so pale, so sad, so wildly?
Telusa. Eurota, the game I follow is the thing I fly; my strange
disease my chief desire.   35

---

17. *made*] (*a*) thought to be; (*b*) created. The paradoxical nature of chastity,
as described in the following lines, contributes to the universal 'doubleness' of
the play world. See Introduction, pp. 4ff.

18. *divine*] (*a*) thought to be divine; (*b*) pertaining to the gods.

20. *soundeth*] resounds.

22. *lunary*] moonwort, a shade-loving plant (hence its paradoxical
response to the beams of the sun), thought to have magical properties.

23. *sooner*] more readily.

24. *Melibeus*] the disguised Phillida. See 2.4.3n.

false] break, be false to.

25. *Fond*] Foolish.

26. *profession*] vocation.

27–8. *red mask*] flushed appearance (as if from hunting).

31. *game . . . roused*] quarry whose pursuit she has instigated (by startling
into flight).

32. *bend . . . bows*] make all our bows ready for hunting by bending and
stringing them.

strings] bow strings.

34. *game*] quarry.

Eurota. I am no Oedipus to expound riddles, and I muse how
thou canst be Sphinx to utter them. But I pray thee,
Telusa, tell me what thou ailest. If thou be sick, this
ground hath leaves to heal; if melancholy, here are pastimes to use; if peevish, wit must wean it, or time, or   40
counsel. If thou be in love (for I have heard of such a
beast called love) it shall be cured. Why blushest thou,
Telusa?

Telusa. To hear thee in reckoning my pains to recite thine own.
I saw, Eurota, how amorously you glanced your eye on   45
the fair boy in the white coat, and how cunningly, now
that you would have some talk of love, you hit me in the
teeth with love.

Eurota. I confess that I am in love, and yet swear that I know
not what it is. I feel my thoughts unknit, mine eyes   50
unstayed, my heart I know not how affected (or infected),
my sleeps broken and full of dreams, my wakeness sad
and full of sighs, myself in all things unlike myself. If this
be love, I would it had never been devised.

Telusa. Thou hast told what I am, in uttering what thyself   55
is. These are my passions, Eurota, my unbridled
passions, my intolerable passions, which I were as
good acknowledge and crave counsel as to deny and
endure peril.

Eurota. How did it take you first, Telusa?   60

36–7. *Oedipus . . . utter them*] A legendary Greek hero, Oedipus delivered
the Thebans from the Sphinx, a she-monster who slew every traveller unable
to solve the riddle that she posed, by answering the puzzle, causing the
Sphinx to take her own life.
38. *what thou ailest*] from what you are suffering.
40. *peevish*] out of temper.
wit . . . it] your rational mind must reason you out of it.
46. *fair . . . coat*] i.e. the disguised Galatea. See line 67 below.
47–8. *hit . . . teeth with*] accuse me of.
50. *unknit*] disjointed.
51. *unstayed*] wandering.
52. *wakeness*] waking hours.
57–8. *were as good*] might as well.

Telusa. By the eyes, my wanton eyes, which conceived the
    picture of his face and hanged it on the very strings of
    my heart. Oh, fair Melibeus! Oh, fond Telusa! But how
    did it take you, Eurota?
Eurota. By the ears, whose sweet words sunk so deep into   65
    my head that the remembrance of his wit hath bereaved
    me of my wisdom. Oh, eloquent Tityrus! Oh, credulous
    Eurota! But soft, here cometh Ramia. But let her not
    hear us talk. We will withdraw ourselves, and hear
    her talk.   [*They stand aside.*]   70

                    Enter RAMIA.

Ramia. I am sent to seek others that have lost myself.
Eurota. [*To Telusa*] You shall see Ramia hath also bitten on a
    love-leaf.
Ramia. Can there be no heart so chaste but love can wound,
    nor vows so holy but affection can violate? Vain art thou,   75
    virtue, and thou, chastity, but a byword, when you both
    are subject to love, of all things the most abject. If love
    be a god, why should not lovers be virtuous? Love *is* a
    god, and lovers *are* virtuous.

            [EUROTA *and* TELUSA *come forward.*]

Eurota. Indeed, Ramia, if lovers were not virtuous, then wert   80
    thou vicious.
Ramia. What, are you come so near me?
Telusa. I think we came near you when we said you loved.

---

61. *By the eyes*] the traditional route by which the affections were thought
to be engaged. Cf. *The Merchant of Venice*: 'Tell me where is Fancy bred, /
Or in the heart, or in the head? . . . / It is engend'red in the eyes'
(3.2.63–7).
67. *Tityrus*] the disguised Galatea.
68. *soft*] hush.
73. *love-leaf*] love-inducing herb (used metaphorically here).
76. *but a byword*] just a term for something to be scorned.
77. *abject*] debased.
81. *vicious*] given to vice.
82. *are you . . . me*] (*a*) are you so close to me (the sense that Ramia
intends); (*b*) do you understand me so well (the meaning Telusa plays on in
the following line).

Eurota. Tush, Ramia, 'Tis too late to recall it; to repent it a
    shame. Therefore, I pray thee, tell what is love.   85
Ramia. If myself felt only this infection, I would then take upon
    me the definition, but being incident to so many I dare not
    myself describe it. But we will all talk of that in the woods.
    Diana stormeth that, sending one to seek another, she
    loseth all. Servia, of all the nymphs the coyest, loveth   90
    deadly, and exclaimeth against Diana, honoureth Venus,
    detesteth Vesta, and maketh a common scorn of virtue.
    Clymene, whose stately looks seemed to amaze the greatest
    lords, stoopeth, yieldeth, and fawneth on the strange boy
    in the woods. Myself (with blushing I speak it) am thrall   95
    to that boy, that fair boy, that beautiful boy!
Telusa. What have we here? All in love? No other food than
    fancy? No, no, she shall not have the fair boy!
Eurota. Nor you, Telusa!
Ramia. Nor you, Eurota!   100
Telusa. I love Melibeus, and my deserts shall be answerable
    to my desires. I will forsake Diana for him. I will die for
    him!
Ramia. So saith Clymene, and she will have him. I care not.
    My sweet Tityrus, though he seem proud, I impute it to   105
    childishness, who, being scarce out of his swath-clouts,
    cannot understand these deep conceits. I love him!
Eurota. So do I, and I will have him!

---

84. *Tush*] dismissive exclamation.
86. *myself felt only*] I were the only one to feel.
89. *stormeth*] rages.
90. *coyest*] most disdainful of love.
91. *deadly*] to a desperate extreme.
92. *Vesta*] See line 11n. above.
maketh . . . virtue] holds virtue up to public derision.
93. *amaze*] confound.
95–6. *thrall to*] captivated by.
96. *that fair boy*] ambiguous, as the following lines reveal, in that each
nymph believes her to be speaking of the boy she loves.
101–2. *my deserts . . . my desires*] the reward I will merit will correspond
with that which I desire.
106. *swath-clouts*] cloths in which new-born infants were wrapped.
107. *conceits*] concepts.

Telusa. Immodest all that we are, unfortunate all that we
are like to be. Shall virgins begin to wrangle for love,   110
and become wanton in their thoughts, in their words, in
their actions? O divine love, which art therefore called
divine because thou overreachest the wisest, conquerest
the chastest, and dost all things most unlikely and
impossible, because thou art love! Thou makest the   115
bashful, impudent; the wise, fond; the chaste, wanton;
and workest contraries to our reach, because thyself is
beyond reason.
Eurota. Talk no more, Telusa; your words wound. Ah, would
I were no woman!   120
Ramia. Would Tityrus were no boy!
Telusa. Would Telusa were nobody!   *Exeunt.*

3.2.   [*Enter*] PHILLIDA *and* GALATEA.

Phillida. It is pity that Nature framed you not a woman,
having a face so fair, so lovely a countenance, so modest
a behaviour.
Galatea. There is a tree in Tylos, whose nuts have shells like
fire, and, being cracked, the kernel is but water.   5
Phillida. What a toy is it to tell me of that tree, being nothing
to the purpose! I say it is pity you are not a woman.
Galatea. I would not wish to be a woman, unless it were
because thou art a man.
Phillida. Nay, I do not wish [thee] to be a woman, for then I   10
should not love thee. For I have sworn never to love a
woman.

---

111. *wanton*] ungoverned.
113. *thou overreachest*] you out-wit.
116. *fond*] foolish.
wanton] lascivious.
117. *workest . . . reach*] effect impossible things beyond our capabilities or
imagining.
117–18. *thyself . . . reason*] your operations lie outside the realm of the
rational.

1. *framed you not*] did not make you.
4. *a tree in Tylos*] No source has been traced for this reference.
6. *toy*] pointless thing.
10. *thee*] omitted from the earliest editions.

Galatea. A strange humour in so pretty a youth, and according to mine, for myself will never love a woman.

Phillida. It were a shame, if a maiden should be a suitor (a   15
thing hated in that sex), that thou shouldst deny to be her servant.

Galatea. If it be a shame in me, it can be no commendation in you, for yourself is of that mind.

Phillida. Suppose I were a virgin (I blush in supposing myself   20
one), and that under the habit of a boy were the person of a maid, if I should utter my affection with sighs, manifest my sweet love by my salt tears, and prove my loyalty unspotted and my griefs intolerable, would not then that fair face pity this true heart?   25

Galatea. Admit that I were as you would have me suppose that you are, and that I should with entreaties, prayers, oaths, bribes, and whatever can be invented in love, desire your favour, would you not yield?

Phillida. Tush, you come in with 'admit'.   30

Galatea. And you with 'suppose'.

Phillida. [*Aside*] What doubtful speeches be these! I fear me he is as I am, a maiden.

Galatea. [*Aside*] What dread riseth in my mind! I fear the boy to be as I am, a maiden.   35

Phillida. [*Aside*] Tush, it cannot be; his voice shows the contrary.

Galatea. [*Aside*] Yet I do not think it; for he would then have blushed.

Phillida. Have you ever a sister?   40

---

13. *humour*] whim, inclination.

13–14. *according to*] in accordance with.

16–17. *deny . . . servant*] refuse to be her devoted lover. The terms 'servant' and 'mistress' denoted the relationship between a lover and his lady in the courtly love tradition.

19. *yourself . . . mind*] you have made the same decision.

21. *habit*] garments.

23–4. *prove . . . unspotted*] show my faith to be untarnished.

32. *doubtful*] ambiguous.

40–4.] The evasive exchange here is echoed by Shakespeare in a scene between Orsino and the disguised Viola in *Twelfth Night* (2.4.108–10).

40. *ever a sister*] any sisters.

Galatea. If I had but one, my brother must needs have two. But, I pray, have you ever a one?

Phillida. My father had but one daughter, and therefore I could have no sister.

Galatea. [*Aside*] Ay me! He is as I am, for his speeches be as   45
mine are.

Phillida. [*Aside*] What shall I do? Either he is subtle or my sex simple.

Galatea. [*Aside*] I have known divers of Diana's nymphs enamoured of him, yet hath he rejected all, either as too   50
proud, to disdain, or too childish, not to understand, or for that he knoweth himself to be a virgin.

Phillida. [*Aside*] I am in a quandary! Diana's nymphs have followed him and he despised them, either knowing too well the beauty of his own face, or that himself is of the   55
same mould. I will once again try him. [*To Galatea*] You promised me in the woods that you would love me before all Diana's nymphs.

Galatea. Ay, so you would love me before all Diana's nymphs.   60

Phillida. Can you prefer a fond boy, as I am, before so fair ladies, as they are?

Galatea. Why should not I as well as you?

Phillida. Come, let us into the grove, and make much of one another, that cannot tell what to think of one   65
another.   *Exeunt.*

3.3.   [*Enter the*] ALCHEMIST [*and*] RAFE.

Alchemist. Rafe, my boy is run away. I trust thou wilt not run after.

---

42. *ever a one*] any.

45. *Ay me*] Alas.

47–8. *my sex simple*] women are not very astute.

49. *divers*] several.

50–1. *too proud ... understand*] disdainful through excessive pride, or uncomprehending through extreme youth.

56. *mould*] cast, shape.

59. *so*] provided that.

61. *fond*] foolish.

1. *boy*] young servant (i.e. Peter).

Rafe. [*Aside*] I would I had a pair of wings, that I might fly after.

Alchemist. My boy was the veriest thief, the arrantest liar, and
the vilest swearer in the world, otherwise the best boy in   5
the world. He hath stolen my apparel, all my money, and
forgot nothing but to bid me farewell.

Rafe. That will not I forget. Farewell, master!

Alchemist. Why, thou hast not yet seen the end of my art.

Rafe. I would I had not known the beginning. Did not you   10
promise me of my silver thimble to make a whole cupboard of plate, and that of a Spanish needle you would
build a silver steeple?

Alchemist. Ay, Rafe, the fortune of this art consisteth in the
measure of the fire, for if there be a coal too much or a   15
spark too little, if it be a little too hot or a thought too
soft, all our labour is in vain. Besides, they that blow must
beat time with their breaths, as musicians do with their
breasts, so as there must be of the metals, the fire, and
workers a very harmony.   20

Rafe. Nay, if you must weigh your fire by ounces, and take
measure of a man's blast, you may then make of a dram
of wind a wedge of gold, and of the shadow of one shilling
make another, so as you have an organist to tune your
temperatures.   25

---

4. *veriest*] most thoroughgoing.

arrantest] most downright.

9. *end*] (*a*) outcome (the sense the Alchemist intends); (*b*) conclusion (the
meaning Rafe plays on in the following line).

12. *plate*] silver tableware.

Spanish needle] Spain was renowned during this period for the production
of metalware.

14. *fortune*] success.

15. *measure*] precise proportions.

17. *soft*] moderate.

19. *breasts*] voices (in singing).

20. *very*] true.

21-2. *weigh . . . blast*] an echo of the proverbial expression, 'To weigh the
fire and measure the wind', signifying to attempt the impossible.

22. *blast*] breath.

dram] a minute measure of weight (a sixteenth of an ounce avoirdupois).

23. *shilling*] twelve pence in pre-decimalization English currency. A skilled
man earned between six and eight shillings a week.

24. *organist*] (*a*) one who organizes the performance of a melody; (*b*) one
who plays a musical instrument, specifically the organ.

Alchemist. So is it; and often doth it happen that the just
    proportion of the fire and all things concur.
Rafe. Concur? Condog! I will away!
Alchemist. Then away!   *Exit* [*the*] ALCHEMIST.

                Enter [*an*] ASTRONOMER [*abstracted*].

Rafe. An art, quoth you, that one multiplieth so much all day   30
    that he wanteth money to buy meat at night! [*He sees the
    Astronomer.*] But what have we yonder? What devout
    man? He will never speak till he be urged. I will salute
    him. – Sir, there lieth a purse under your feet. If I thought
    it were not yours, I would take it up.   35
Astronomer. Dost thou not know that I was calculating the
    nativity of Alexander's great horse?
Rafe. Why, what are you?
Astronomer. An astronomer.
Rafe. What, one of those that makes almanacs?   40
Astronomer. *Ipsissimus*! I can tell the minute of thy birth, the
    moment of thy death, and the manner. I can tell thee

---

27. *concur*] come together.

28. *Condog*] meaningless exclamation repudiating the Alchemist's service,
punning on *concur* in the previous line.

30. *quoth you*] you say (used derisively here).

31. *wanteth*] lacks.

meat] food.

32. *devout*] The description suggests that the Astronomer enters consult-
ing a book, which Rafe takes to be a Bible.

34–5. *Sir . . . up*] While functioning as a means of allowing Rafe to engage
in conversation with the Astronomer, the dropping of the purse signals the
spuriousness of the latter's claim that 'Nothing can happen which I foresee
not' (lines 48–9 below).

36–7. *calculating the nativity*] working out the position of the stars at the
moment of birth in order to construct a horoscope.

37. *Alexander's great horse*] Bucephalus, legendary mount of Alexander the
Great.

39. *astronomer*] astrologer. Astronomy and astrology were not differenti-
ated as distinct branches of study in the sixteenth century.

40. *almanacs*] popular calendars (published annually) listing the months
and days, and including a wealth of astrological and astronomical information.

41. Ipsissimus] the very man (Latin). The following description of the
Astronomer's 'science' confirms that he is an astrologer rather than an
astronomer, as those terms are understood today.

42. *manner*] way in which you will die.

what weather shall be between this and *octogessimus*
octavus mirabilis annus. When I list, I can set a trap for the
sun, catch the moon with lime-twigs, and go a-batfowling   45
for stars. I can tell thee things past, and things to come,
and with my cunning measure how many yards of clouds
are beneath the sky. Nothing can happen which I foresee
not; nothing shall.

Rafe. I hope, sir, you are no more than a god?   50

Astronomer. I can bring the twelve signs out of their zodiacs,
and hang them up at taverns.

Rafe. I pray you, sir, tell me what you cannot do, for I perceive
there is nothing so easy for you to compass as impossibilities. But what be those signs?   55

Astronomer. As a man should say, signs which govern the body.
The Ram governeth the head.

Rafe. That is the worst sign for the head.

Astronomer. Why?

Rafe. Because it is a sign of an ill ewe.   60

Astronomer. Tush, that sign must be there. Then the Bull for
the throat, Capricornus for the knees.

---

43. *this*] this time.

43-4. octogessimus . . . annus] the wonderful year of eighty-eight (Latin).
A prophecy regarding the eighty-eighth year had been in circulation since
the fifteenth century and was taken at the close of the sixteenth century to
refer to the defeat of the Spanish Armada in 1588. Both the composition of
Lyly's play and its performance at court antedate the Spanish defeat, but
would have lent topicality to its publication in 1592.

44. *list*] wish.

45. *lime-twigs*] twigs smeared with a sticky lime, designed to catch small birds.

45-6. *a-batfowling for stars*] catching (literally 'beating down') stars by night
as if they were roosting birds (from Middle English *bat* = beat + *fowl* = bird).

51. *twelve signs*] the symbols of the twelve equal divisions of the zodiac,
through each of which the sun passes in turn.

52. *hang . . . taverns*] a reference to the frequent use of celestial bodies for
inn signs, e.g. the Bull (i.e. Taurus).

56. *signs . . . body*] Each of the twelve signs of the zodiac was thought to
govern a particular part of the human frame, in accordance with the notion
of a single order pervading creation as a whole.

57. *The Ram*] Aries.

60. *ill ewe*] unfaithful wife. The joke turns upon the conventional association
between horns (here the horns of the ram) and cuckoldry.

61. *the Bull*] Taurus.

62. *Capricornus*] the sign of the goat.

Rafe. I will hear no more of these signs, if they be all such
desperate signs. But seeing you are – I know not who to
term you – shall I serve you? I would fain serve.   65
Astronomer. I accept thee.
Rafe. Happy am I, for now I shall read thoughts, and tell how
many drops of water goes to the greatest shower of rain.
You shall see me catch the moon in the clips, like a cony
in a purse-net.   70
Astronomer. I will teach thee the golden number, the epact,
and the prime.
Rafe. I will meddle no more with numbering of gold,
for multiplication is a miserable action. I pray, sir,
what weather shall we have this hour threescore   75
year?
Astronomer. That must be cast by our judicials astronomical.
Therefore come in with me, and thou shall see every
wrinkle of my astrological wisdom, and I will make the
heavens as plain to thee as the highway. Thy cunning shall   80
sit cheek by jowl with the sun's chariot. Then shalt thou

---

64. *desperate*] discouraging, offering no hope.

65. *fain*] gladly.

69. *clips*] eclipse.

cony] rabbit.

70. *purse-net*] bag-shaped net, drawn in at the neck with a cord.

71. *golden number*] the number of any year in the lunar cycle of nineteen
years relative to the moon's return to its starting point in relation to the sun.
The numbers (used in determining the date of Easter) were inscribed in gold
in the margins of ecclesiastical calendars.

epact] the age of the moon (in days) on the first day of the year (22 March
in the Julian calendar, still in force for some purposes when the play was
composed). The term was also used for the difference in length between the
solar and lunar years.

72. *prime*] the beginning of any astronomical period or cycle, specifically
the first appearance of the new moon.

74. *multiplication*] the increase of gold through an alchemical process, i.e.
the project on which the Alchemist was engaged.

75–6. *this . . . year*] at this time sixty years from now.

77. *judicials astronomical*] predictions regarding the course of future events
by reference to the disposition of heavenly bodies.

79. *wrinkle*] detail.

80. *cunning*] knowledge.

81. *sit . . . chariot*] be situated side by side with the vehicle of Apollo (i.e.
range through the heavens like the sun).

see what a base thing it is to have others' thoughts creep
on the ground, whenas thine shall be stitched to the stars.
Rafe. Then I shall be translated from this mortality!
Astronomer. Thy thoughts shall be metamorphosed, and made   85
hail-fellows with the gods.
Rafe. O fortune! I feel my very brains moralized, and as it
were a certain contempt of earthly actions is crept into
my mind by an ethereal contemplation. Come, let us
in!   *Exeunt.*   90

3.4.   [*Enter*] DIANA, TELUSA, EUROTA, RAMIA,
                           [*and*] LARISSA.

Diana. What news have we here, ladies? Are all in love? Are
Diana's nymphs become Venus' wantons? Is it a shame
to be chaste because you be amiable, or must you needs
be amorous because you are fair? O Venus, if this be thy
spite I will requite it with more than hate. Well shalt thou   5
know what it is to drib thine arrows up and down Diana's
leas. There is an unknown nymph that straggleth up and
down these woods, which I suspect hath been the weaver
of these woes. I saw her slumbering by the brook side.
Go search her, and bring her. If you find upon her shoul-   10
der a burn, it is Cupid; if any print on her back like a

<hr>

83. *whenas*] when.
84. *translated . . . mortality*] lifted up from the human condition.
85–6. *made hail-fellows*] put on terms of easy acquaintance.
87. *moralized*] infused with a more elevated understanding.
89. *ethereal*] sublime, other worldly.

3. *amiable*] beautiful.
6. *drib thine arrows*] shoot your arrows wide or short of the mark.
7. *leas*] meadows.
straggleth] wanders.
10. *search*] seek.
10–11. *If you . . . burn*] a reference to the scar caused by the drop of oil
from Psyche's lamp that fell on the shoulder of her lover (Cupid) when she
rose in the night to regard him. The allusion complicates the construction
of Cupid, who is otherwise presented as a mischievous boy, rather than a
young man (cf. 5.3.93ff.).

leaf, it is Medea; if any picture on her left breast like a
bird, it is Calypso. Whoever it be, bring her hither, and
speedily bring her hither.
Telusa. I will go with speed.   15
Diana. Go you, Larissa, and help her.
Larissa. I obey.   [*Exeunt* TELUSA *and* LARISSA.]
Diana. Now, ladies, doth not that make your cheeks blush,
that makes mine ears glow; or can you remember that
without sobs, which Diana cannot think on without sighs?   20
What greater dishonour could happen to Diana, or to her
nymphs shame, than that there can be any time so idle
that should make their heads so addle? Your chaste hearts,
my nymphs, should resemble the onyx, which is hottest
when it is whitest, and your thoughts, the more they are   25
assaulted with desires, the less they should be affected.
You should think love like Homer's moly, a white leaf
and a black root, a fair show and a bitter taste. Of all trees
the cedar is greatest and hath the smallest seeds; of
all affections love hath the greatest name and the least   30
virtue. Shall it be said, and shall Venus say it – nay, shall
it be seen, and shall wantons see it – that Diana, the
goddess of chastity, whose thoughts are always answerable to her vows, whose eyes never glanced on desire, and
whose heart abateth the point of Cupid's arrows, shall   35

11–12. *if any . . . Medea*] No source has been traced for the distinguishing
mark, which alludes to the extensive herb-lore for which Medea, lover of
Jason, was renowned.

12–13. *if any . . . Calypso*] Having fallen in love with Odysseus, Calypso
sought, in vain, to detain him with the promise of immortality. The picture
of a bird on her left breast (which appears to be Lyly's invention) may refer
to the birds that flew around her cave.

22. *any time so idle*] Idleness was traditionally regarded as a prime instiga-
tor of sexual love.

23. *addle*] confused, unsound.

24. *onyx*] a variety of quartz, to which a number of fabulous properties
were ascribed.

27. *Homer's moly*] fabulous plant with white flowers and black root, said
by Homer to have been given by Hermes to Odysseus as a charm against
the sorceress, Circe.

30. *name*] reputation.

33–4. *answerable to*] in accordance with.

35. *abateth*] blunts.

have her virgins to become unchaste in desires, immoder-
ate in affection, untemperate in love, in foolish love, in
base love? Eagles cast their evil feathers in the sun, but
you cast your best desires upon a shadow. The birds ibes
lose their sweetness when they lose their sights, and   40
virgins all their virtues with their unchaste thoughts –
'unchaste' Diana calleth that that hath either any show or
suspicion of lightness. Oh, my dear nymphs, if you knew
how loving thoughts stain lovely faces, you would be as
careful to have the one as unspotted as the other   45
beautiful.
      Cast before your eyes the loves of Venus' trulls, their
fortunes, their fancies, their ends. What are they else but
Silenus' pictures – without, lambs and doves; within, apes
and owls – who, like Ixion, embrace clouds for Juno, the   50
shadows of virtue instead of the substance? The eagle's
feathers consume the feathers of all others, and love's
desire corrupteth all other virtues. I blush, ladies, that
you, having been heretofore patient of labours, should
now become prentices to idleness and use the pen for   55

---

37. *untemperate*] inwardly disordered.

38. *Eagles . . . sun*] a reference to the popular belief that eagles, bedraggled
with old age, fly up towards the sun to heat themselves and then plunge
down into the water beneath them, where their feathers are renewed and
their youth restored.

39–40. *The birds . . . sights*] a reference to the ibis (plural *ibes*), reputed to
smell sweeter with advancing age. No source has been traced, however, for
the loss of its pleasant smell with the failure of its sight.

43. *lightness*] sexual misconduct, immodesty.

47. *trulls*] wantons, strumpets (with the implication here of devotees).

48. *ends*] fates.

49–50. *Silenus' . . . owls*] a reversal of Athenian depictions of the grotesque
satyr Silenus which could be opened to reveal pictures of the gods. The dual
facets of similar images are alluded to in Lyly's first play, *Campaspe* (Prologue
at the Court, lines 2–5).

50. *Ixion . . . Juno*] attempting to seduce Juno, Ixion embraced a phantom
created by Jove in her place, and was punished for his presumption by being
chained to an ever-turning wheel.

51–2. *eagle's . . . others*] Eagles' feathers were reputed to destroy those of
any other bird which came into contact with them.

54. *heretofore . . . labours*] content to endure toil before this.

55. *prentices to idleness*] bound to an idle condition (*prentices* =
apprentices).

sonnets, not the needle for samplers. And how is your
love placed? Upon pelting boys, perhaps base of birth,
without doubt weak of discretion. Ay, but they are fair!
Oh, ladies, do your eyes begin to love colours, whose
hearts was wont to loathe them? Is Diana's chase become   60
Venus' court, and are your holy vows turned to hollow
thoughts?

Ramia. Madam, if love were not a thing beyond reason, we
might then give a reason for our doings, but so divine is
his force that it worketh effects as contrary to that we   65
wish as unreasonable against that we ought.

[Eurota]. Lady, so unacquainted are the passions of love that
we can neither describe them nor bear them.

Diana. Foolish girls, how willing you are to follow that which
you should fly! But here cometh Telusa.   70

Enter TELUSA *and* [LARISSA,] *with* CUPID.

Telusa. We have brought the disguised nymph, and have found
on his shoulder Psyche's burn, and he confesses himself
to be Cupid.

Diana. How now, sir, are you caught? Are you Cupid?

Cupid. Thou shalt see, Diana, that I dare confess myself to be   75
Cupid.

Diana. And thou shalt see, Cupid, that I will show myself to
be Diana, that is, conqueror of thy loose and untamed
appetites. Did thy mother, Venus, under the colour of a
nymph send thee hither to wound my nymphs? Doth she   80
add craft to her malice, and, mistrusting her deity, practise deceit? Is there no place but my groves, no persons

56. *samplers*] See 2.4.12n.
57. *pelting*] paltry.
58. *weak of discretion*] lacking in judgement.
59. *colours*] appearances.
60. *chase*] hunting ground.
67. Eurota] The speech is wrongly ascribed to the absent Larissa in the
earliest edition.
unacquainted] unfamiliar.
72. *Psyche's burn*] See lines 10–11n. above.
79. *colour*] disguise, outward appearance.
81–2. *mistrusting . . . deceit*] lacking faith in her power as a goddess, engage
in deception.

but my nymphs? Cruel and unkind Venus, that spiteth
only chastity, thou shalt see that Diana's power shall
revenge thy policy, and tame this pride. As for thee,   85
Cupid, I will break thy bow and burn thine arrows, bind
thy hands, clip thy wings, and fetter thy feet. Thou that
fattest others with hopes shalt be fed thyself upon wishes,
and thou that bindest others with golden thoughts shalt
be bound thyself with golden fetters. Venus' rods are   90
made of roses, Diana's of briars. Let Venus, that great
goddess, ransom Cupid, that little god. These ladies here,
whom thou hast infected with foolish love, shall both
tread on thee and triumph over thee. Thine own arrow
shall be shot into thine own bosom, and thou shalt be   95
enamoured not on Psyches, but on Circes. I will teach
thee what it is to displease Diana, distress her nymphs,
or disturb her game.

Cupid. Diana, what I have done cannot be undone, but what
you mean to do, shall. Venus hath some gods to her   100
friends. Cupid shall have all!

Diana. Are you prating? I will bridle thy tongue and thy
power, and in spite of mine own thoughts I will set thee
a task every day, which if thou finish not thou shalt feel
the smart. Thou shalt be used as Diana's slave, not Venus'   105
son. All the world shall see that I will use thee like a
captive, and show myself a conqueror. [*To her nymphs*]
Come, have him in, that we may devise apt punishments
for his proud presumptions.

83–4. *spiteth only*] is malicious only towards.

85. *policy*] plotting.

88. *fattest*] feeds.

wishes] hopes of release.

90. *rods*] canes (used for punishment).

96. *Psyches / Circes*] Psyche epitomizes devoted love through the suffering
she endured for Cupid's sake, Circe demeaning enchantment through her
transformation of the followers of Odysseus into swine.

98. *game*] sport.

101. *all*] (*a*) all the gods (in his support); (*b*) the ultimate victory.

102. *prating*] chattering, being insolent.

bridle] curb (metaphor drawn from the management of horses).

103. *in spite . . . thoughts*] for all my reluctance to engage with you.

Eurota. We will plague ye for a little god.   110
Telusa. We will never pity thee, though thou be a god.
Ramia. Nor I.
Larissa. Nor I.   *Exeunt.*

Act 4

4.1. [*Enter*] AUGUR, MELIBEUS, TITYRUS,
[*and a number of their fellow countrymen*].

Augur. This is the day wherein you must satisfy Neptune and
save yourselves. Call together your fair daughters, and for
a sacrifice take the fairest, for better it is to offer a virgin
than suffer ruin. If you think it against nature to sacrifice
your children, think it also against sense to destroy your   5
country. If you imagine Neptune pitiless to desire such a
prey, confess yourselves perverse to deserve such a punishment. You see this tree, this fatal tree, whose leaves,
though they glister like gold, yet it threateneth to fair
virgins grief? To this tree must the beautifullest be bound   10
until the monster, Agar, carry her away, and if the monster
come not, then assure yourselves that the fairest is con-
cealed, and then your country shall be destroyed. Therefore consult with yourselves, not as fathers of children,
but as favourers of your country. Let Neptune have his   15
right, if you will have your quiet. Thus have I warned you
to be careful, and would wish you to be wise, knowing
that whoso hath the fairest daughter hath the greatest
fortune, in losing one to save all. And so I depart to
provide ceremonies for the sacrifice, and command you   20
to bring the sacrifice.   *Exit* AUGUR.
Melibeus. They say, Tityrus, that you have a fair daughter. If
it be so, dissemble not, for you shall be a fortunate father.
It is a thing holy to preserve one's country, and honourable to be the cause.   25

---

1. *wherein*] on which.
11. *the monster, Agar*] See 1.1.52ff.
15–16. *his right*] that which is due to him.
16. *will*] wish to.
23. *dissemble not*] do not pretend otherwise.
fortunate] blessed (in being the one to preserve his community).

89

Tityrus. Indeed, Melibeus, I have heard you boast that you
had a fair daughter, than the which none was more beautiful. I hope that you are not so careful of a child that you
will be careless of your country, or add so much to nature
that you will detract from wisdom.   30
Melibeus. I must confess that I had a daughter, and I know
you have; but, alas, my child's cradle was her grave, and
her swath-clout her winding-sheet. I would she had lived
till now; she should willingly have died now. For what
could have happened to poor Melibeus more comfortable   35
than to be the father of a fair child and sweet country.
Tityrus. Oh, Melibeus, dissemble you may with men; deceive
the gods you cannot. Did not I see (and very lately see)
your daughter in your arms, whenas you gave her infinite
kisses, with affection (I fear me) more than fatherly? You   40
have conveyed her away, that you might cast us all away,
bereaving her the honour of her beauty and us the benefit,
preferring a common inconvenience before a private
mischief.
Melibeus. It is a bad cloth, Tityrus, that will take no colour,   45
and a simple father that can use no cunning. You make
the people believe that you wish well when you practise

---

28. *careful of*] full of care for.
29. *be careless of*] lack regard for.
add so much to nature] so exceed (in fatherly love) that which the bonds
of kinship dictate.
30. *detract from wisdom*] impair your judgement.
33. *swath-clout*] swaddling bands (i.e. the cloth in which she was wrapped
at birth).
winding-sheet] shroud.
35. *comfortable*] agreeable, satisfying.
39. *whenas*] when.
41. *conveyed*] stolen.
cast . . . away] destroy us all.
42. *bereaving her*] depriving her of.
43. *common inconvenience*] public misfortune.
43-4. *private mischief*] personal affliction.
45. *It is . . . colour*] a proverbial expression, drawn from the dyeing of cloth,
signifying that any cause is capable of justification, however specious.
take no colour] entirely resist the dye.
46. *simple*] very weak-witted.
cunning] guile.
47. *practise*] engage in.

nothing but ill, wishing to be thought religious towards
the gods when I know you deceitful towards men. You
cannot overreach me, Tityrus; overshoot yourself you   50
may. It is a wily mouse that will breed in the cat's ear,
and he must halt cunningly that will deceive a cripple.
Did you ever see me kiss my daughter? You are deceived;
it was my wife. And if you thought so young a piece unfit
for so old a person, and therefore imagined it to be my   55
child, not my spouse, you must know that silver hairs
delight in golden locks, and the old fancies crave young
nurses, and frosty years must be thawed by youthful fires.
But this matter set aside, you have a fair daughter, Tityrus,
and it is pity you are so fond a father.   60
First countryman. You are both either too fond or too froward;
for whilst you dispute to save your daughters, we neglect
to prevent our destruction.
Second countryman. Come, let us away and seek out a sacrifice. We must sift out their cunning, and let them shift for   65
themselves.   *Exeunt.*

4.2.   *Enter* TELUSA, EUROTA, [*and*] LARISSA, *singing,*
                    [*with*] CUPID [*and* RAMIA].

Telusa.   Oyez, oyez, if any maid
                 Whom leering Cupid has betrayed

---

50. *overreach*] outwit.
overshoot yourself] exceed your own capabilities.
51. *It is . . . ear*] a proverbial expression used in relation to those foolishly
flattering themselves on their courage or guile.
52. *he must . . . cripple*] another proverbial analogy used with reference to
a person attempting to deceive someone better informed than himself.
halt cunningly] limp skilfully.
54. *piece*] person.
57. *fancies*] appetites.
60. *fond*] doting (also at line 61 below).
61. *froward*] recalcitrant, perverse.
65. *sift out*] look into.
shift for] look after.

1–20.] See 1.4.87–105n. for the textual history of the play's songs.
1. *Oyez, oyez*] Hear ye, hear ye (the traditional call of the town crier or court
official, summoning the populace in order to impart information or news).
2. *leering*] sidelong-glancing (with lascivious overtones).

	To frowns of spite, to eyes of scorn,	
	And would in madness now see torn	
	The boy in pieces –	
All 3.	Let her come	5
	Hither, and lay on him her doom.	

Eurota.   Oyez, oyez, has any lost
              A heart which many a sigh hath cost?
              Is any cozened of a tear,
              Which, as a pearl, Disdain does wear?   10
              Here stands the thief –
All 3.   Let her but come
              Hither, and lay on him her doom.

Larissa.   Is anyone undone by fire,
              And turned to ashes through desire?
              Did ever any lady weep,   15
              Being cheated of her golden sleep,
              Stolen by sick thoughts?
All 3.   The pirate's found,
              And in her tears he shall be drowned!
              Read his indictment, let him hear
              What he's to trust to. Boy, give ear!   20

Telusa. Come, Cupid, to your task. First you must undo all
    these lovers' knots, because you tied them.
                    [She indicates a pile of love-knots.]
Cupid. If they be true love-knots, 'tis unpossible to unknit
    them; if false, I never tied them.
Eurota. Make no excuse, but to it.   25

---

    3. *spite*] vexation.
    6. *doom*] judgement (also at line 12 below).
    9. *cozened*] cheated.
    13. *fire*] the flames of love.
    20. *trust to*] look for.
    give ear] listen.
    22. *lovers' knots*] bows, usually of ribbon, tied in a particular way, signify-
ing the indissolubility of the relationship between the parties.
    23. *unknit*] untie, loosen.
    25. *to it*] begin (also at line 30 below).

Cupid. Love-knots are tied with eyes, and cannot be undone
    with hands; made fast with thoughts, and cannot be
    unloosed with fingers. Had Diana no other task to set
    Cupid to but things impossible? [*They threaten him.*] I will
    to it.   [*He sets to work on a love-knot.*]   30
Ramia. Why, how now? You tie the knots faster.
Cupid. I cannot choose. It goeth against my mind to make
    them loose.
Eurota. Let me see. [*She examines the knot.*] Now 'tis unpos-
    sible to be undone!   35
Cupid. It is the true love-knot of a woman's heart, therefore
    cannot be undone.   [*He picks up another knot.*]
Ramia. That falls in sunder of itself.
Cupid. It was made of a man's thought, which will never hang
    together.   [*He sets to work on another knot.*]   40
Larissa. You have undone that well.
Cupid. Ay, because it was never tied well.
Telusa. To the rest, for she will give you no rest. [*Cupid works
    at two more knots.*] These two knots are finely untied.
Cupid. It was because I never tied them. The one was knit by   45
    Pluto, not Cupid, by money, not love; the other by force,
    not faith, by appointment, not affection.
                              [*He puts a knot to one side.*]
Ramia. Why do you lay that knot aside?
Cupid. For death.
Telusa. Why?   50
Cupid. Because the knot was knit by faith, and must only be
    unknit by death.   [*He takes up another knot and laughs.*]
Eurota. Why laugh you?

---

26. *Love-knots . . . eyes*] See 3.1.61n.
31. *faster*] more tightly.
32. *goeth . . . mind*] is contrary to my disposition.
38. *in . . . itself*] apart of its own volition.
39–40. *hang together*] remain constant.
44. *finely*] very well.
46. *Pluto*] the giver of wealth in Greek mythology.
force] compulsion.
47. *appointment*] arrangement.

Cupid. Because it is the fairest and the falsest, done with the
greatest art and least truth, with best colours and worst   55
conceits.

Telusa. Who tied it?

Cupid. A man's tongue.

[*He slips another knot into the front of Larissa's dress.*]

Larissa. Why do you put that in my bosom?

Cupid. Because it is only for a woman's bosom.   60

Larissa. Why, what is it?

Cupid. A woman's heart.

Telusa. Come, let us go in and tell that Cupid hath done his
task. Stay you behind, Larissa, and see he sleep not, for
love will be idle. And take heed you surfeit not, for love   65
will be wanton.

Larissa. Let me alone. I will find him somewhat to do.

                    Exit TELUSA [, RAMIA *and* EUROTA].

Cupid. Lady, can you for pity see Cupid thus punished?

Larissa. Why did Cupid punish us without pity?

Cupid. Is love a punishment?   70

Larissa. It is no pastime.

Cupid. Oh, Venus, if thou sawest Cupid as a captive, bound
to obey that was wont to command, fearing ladies' threats
that once pierced their hearts, I cannot tell whether thou
wouldst revenge it for despite or laugh at it for disport.   75
The time may come, Diana, and the time shall come, that
thou that settest Cupid to undo knots shall entreat Cupid

---

55. *best colours*] the finest show.

56. *conceits*] designs.

65. *love will be idle*] See 3.4.22n.

surfeit not] don't indulge (in his company) to excess.

67. *Let me alone*] Leave it to me.

71. *pastime*] game, pleasurable pursuit.

72–3. *bound to obey*] Compare the predicaments of the sacrificial maiden,
bound to endure the onslaught of the Agar (1.1.56–7) and the three boys
bound to the spar at the mercy of the sea (1.4.6–7).

75. *for despite*] out of indignation.

for disport] as a source of entertainment.

to tie knots – and you ladies that with solace have beheld
my pains shall with sighs entreat my pity.

He offereth to sleep.

Larissa. [*Rousing him*] How now, Cupid, begin you to nod?   80

[*Enter* RAMIA *and* TELUSA.]

Ramia. Come, Cupid, Diana hath devised new labours for
you that are god of loves. You shall weave samplers all
night, and lackey after Diana all day. You shall shortly
shoot at beasts for men, because you have made beasts
of men; and wait on ladies' trains, because thou entrap-   85
pest ladies by trains. All the stories that are in Diana's
arras which are of love you must pick out with your
needle, and in that place sew Vesta with her nuns and
Diana with her nymphs. How like you this, Cupid?

Cupid. I say I will prick as well with my needle as ever I did   90
with mine arrows.

Telusa. Diana cannot yield; she conquers affection.

Cupid. Diana shall yield; she cannot conquer destiny.

Larissa. Come Cupid, you must to your business.

Cupid. You shall find me so busy in your heads that you shall   95
wish I had been idle with your hearts.   *Exeunt.*

---

78. *you ladies*] Addressed to the members of the audience, rather than
Larissa who is alone with Cupid on stage, the comment serves to violate the
boundary between those inside and those outside the play world, inviting
reflection on the pertinence of the drama to its female spectators.

solace] pleasure.

79.1. offereth] makes as if.

80. *How now . . . nod*] See lines 64–5 above.

82. *samplers*] See 2.4.12n.

83. *lackey after Diana*] wait on Diana as a servant.

84. *for*] instead of.

84–5. *made beasts of men*] turned men into beasts (through promoting the
dominance of appetite over reason).

85. *wait . . . trains*] serve those in attendance upon great ladies.

86. *trains*] plots, devices.

87. *arras*] tapestry used as wall hanging.

pick out] unpick.

88. *Vesta . . . nuns*] See 3.1.11n.

94. *business*] task.

95. *busy . . . heads*] active in your thoughts (with a pun on *business* in the
previous line).

4.3.   *[Enter]* NEPTUNE *alone.*

Neptune. [*Approaching the tree*] This day is the solemn sacrifice
at this tree, wherein the fairest virgin (were not the inhabitants faithless) should be offered unto me. But so over-
careful are fathers to their children that they forget the
safety of their country, and, fearing to become unnatural,   5
become unreasonable. Their sleights may blear men;
deceive me they cannot. I will be here at the hour, and
show as great cruelty as they have done craft; and well
shall they know that Neptune should have been entreated,
not cozened.   *Exit.*   10

4.4.   *Enter* GALATEA *and* PHILLIDA.

Phillida. I marvel what virgin the people will present. It is
happy you are none, for then it would have fallen to your
lot, because you are so fair.
Galatea. If you had been a maiden too, I need not to have
feared, because you are fairer.   5
Phillida. I pray thee, sweet boy, flatter not me, speak truth
of thyself; for in mine eye of all the world thou art
fairest.
Galatea. These be fair words, but far from thy true thoughts.
I know mine own face in a true glass, and desire not to   10
see it in a flattering mouth.

---

2. *wherein*] on which.
2–3. *were not . . . faithless*] had the local people not been lacking in piety.
5. *become unnatural*] act contrary to the dictates of nature (in sacrificing
their children).
6. *unreasonable*] blind to what constitutes rational (and thus right)
behaviour.
sleights . . . men] tricks may blur the sight of men.
7. *the hour*] the appointed time.
8. *craft*] cunning.
10. *cozened*] cheated, tricked.

1. *marvel*] wonder.
2. *happy*] fortunate.
none] not a maiden.

Phillida. Oh, would I did flatter thee, and that fortune would
not flatter me! I love thee as a brother; but love not me
so.

Galatea. No, I will not, but love thee better; because I cannot   15
love thee as a brother.

Phillida. Seeing we are both boys, and both lovers, that our
affection may have some show, and seem as it were love,
let me call thee mistress.

Galatea. I accept that name; for divers before have called me   20
mistress.

Phillida. For what cause?

Galatea. Nay, there lie the mysteries.

Phillida. Will not you be at the sacrifice?

Galatea. No.   25

Phillida. Why?

Galatea. Because I dreamed that if I were there I should be
turned to a virgin, and then, being so fair (as thou sayest
I am), I should be offered (as thou knowest one must).
But will not you be there?   30

Phillida. Not unless I were sure that a boy might be sacrificed,
and not a maiden.

Galatea. Why, then you are in danger.

---

12. *flatter thee*] praise your beauty too highly.

13. *flatter me*] encourage me with impossible hopes.

13–14. *love not me so*] do not love me in that way.

17–19.] The proposal looks forward to Shakespeare's *As You Like It*, in
which the disguised Rosalind encourages Orlando to address her as 'Mistress', enabling her to give indirect expression to her love for him. See *As
You Like It*, 3.2.389–423 and 4.1.40ff.

18. *show*] expression.

19, 21, 23. *mistress / mistress / mysteries*] term used by a lover for his lady
in the courtly love tradition / courtesy title used to a woman / plural of
'mystery'. The pun appears more laboured in modern English spelling than
is suggested by the earliest edition, in which the three terms appear as
'Mistris' / 'Mistris' / 'Mistrisse', implying that they were homophones when
the play was composed.

20. *divers*] many.

29. *offered*] sacrificed.

Phillida. But I would escape it by deceit. But seeing we are
resolved to be both absent, let us wander into these groves   35
till the hour be past.

Galatea. I am agreed, for then my fear will be past.

Phillida. Why, what dost thou fear?

Galatea. Nothing, but that you love me not.   *Exit.*

Phillida. I will. – Poor Phillida, what shouldst thou think of   40
thyself, that lovest one that, I fear me, is as thyself is? And
may it not be that her father practised the same deceit
with her that my father hath with me, and, knowing her
to be fair, feared she should be unfortunate? If it be so,
Phillida, how desperate is thy case! If it be not, how   45
doubtful! For if she be a maiden, there is no hope of my
love; if a boy, a hazard. I will after him, or her, and lead
a melancholy life, that look for a miserable death.   *Exit.*

34. *deceit*] dissembling, trickery (an ironic reflection on the fact that she
is actually a girl).

45. *desperate*] hopeless.

46. *doubtful*] uncertain.

47. *a hazard*] only a chance.

48. *that look for*] who expect.

Act 5

5.1.   *Enter* RAFE *alone*.

Rafe. No more masters now, but a mistress, if I can light on
  her. An astronomer! Of all occupations that's the worst.
  Yet well fare the Alchemist, for he keeps good fires though
  he gets no gold; the other stands warming himself by
  staring on the stars, which I think he can as soon number   5
  as know their virtues. He told me a long tale of *octogessimus*
  octavus, and the meeting of the conjunctions and planets,
  and in the meantime he fell backward himself into a pond!
  I asked him why he foresaw not that by the stars. He said
  he knew it, but contemned it! [*He sees someone approach-*   10
  ing.] But soft, is not this my brother, Robin?

                          Enter ROBIN.

Robin. Yes, as sure as thou art Rafe.
Rafe. What, Robin? What news? What fortune?
Robin. Faith, I have had but bad fortune; but, I prithee, tell
  me thine.   15

---

1. *mistress*] (*a*) female employer (the sense Rafe primarily intends); (*b*)
object of a lover's devotion (the sense played on in the second half of the
sentence).
1–2. *if . . . her*] if I can fall in with her (with the bawdy implication 'fall
on her').
3. *well fare*] good luck to.
4. *the other*] the Astronomer.
5. *as soon*] as easily.
number] count.
6. *virtues*] properties.
6–7. octogessimus octavus] See 3.3.43–4n.
8. *and in . . . pond*] the proverbial fate of those professing the power to
foretell the future.
10. *contemned*] scorned.
11. *soft*] just a minute.
14. *but*] nothing but.
prithee] pray thee.

Rafe. I have had two masters, not by art, but by nature. One
said that by multiplying he would make of a penny ten
pound.

Robin. Ay, but could he do it?

Rafe. Could he do it, quoth you? Why, man, I saw a pretty   20
wench come to his shop, where with puffing, blowing,
and sweating, he so plied her that he multiplied her.

Robin. How?

Rafe. Why, he made her of one, two.

Robin. What, by fire?   25

Rafe. No, by the philosopher's stone.

Robin. Why, have philosophers such stones?

Rafe. Ay, but they lie in a privy cupboard.

Robin. Why then, thou art rich if thou have learned this cunning.

Rafe. Tush, this was nothing. He would of a little fasting   30
spittle make a hose and doublet of cloth of silver.

Robin. Would I had been with him, for I have had almost no
meat but spittle since I came to the woods.

Rafe. How, then, didst thou live?

---

16. *not by . . . nature*] (*a*) not because they had academic degrees, but
because they were necessarily masters since I was in their employ; (*b*) not
by design but because that was the customary course of events. The joke
turns on the debate over the relationship between art and nature that was
current when the play was composed.

20. *quoth you*] you say.

22. *so plied her*] worked so vigorously on her (with a bawdy
implication).

multiplied her] The joke turns on the two concepts of multiplication
current when the play was composed: (*a*) increasing the value of materials
through transmutation (i.e. the Alchemist's art); (*b*) a process resulting in an
increase in number (achieved here through pregnancy).

24. *made her of one, two*] i.e. made her pregnant.

26. *the philosopher's stone*] (*a*) the highly prized substance reputed to
change base metals into gold (the sense in which Robin understands the
words); (*b*) the Alchemist's testes (the meaning that Rafe intends).

28. *privy cupboard*] secret storage place (referring here to the scrotum).

29. *cunning*] knowledge.

30–1. *fasting spittle*] saliva taken prior to the first meal of the day.

31. *cloth of silver*] highly prized textile composed of silver threads interwo-
ven with silk or wool.

33. *meat*] food.

spittle] frothy secretion of insects enveloping larvae found on certain plants
(cf. 'cuckoo-spit'), with a pun on *spittle* in line 31 above.

Robin. Why, man, I served a fortune-teller, who said I should   35
    live to see my father hanged, and both my brothers beg.
    So I conclude the mill shall be mine, and live by imagina-
    tion still.

Rafe. Thy master was an ass, and looked on the lines of thy
    hands, but my other master was an astronomer, which   40
    could pick my nativity out of the stars. I should have half
    a dozen stars in my pocket, if I have not lost them. But
    here they be. [*He pulls out a piece of paper and reads.*] 'Sol,
    Saturn, Jupiter, Mars, Venus'.

Robin. Why, these be but names.   45

Rafe. Ay, but by these he gathereth that I was a Jovialist, born
    of a Thursday; and that I should be a brave Venerian, and
    get all my good luck on a Friday.

Robin. 'Tis strange a fish day should be a flesh day.

Rafe. O Robin, *Venus orta mari*; Venus was born of the sea. The   50
    sea will have fish, fish must have wine, wine will have flesh,
    for *caro carnis genus est muliebre*. But soft, here cometh that
    notable villain that once preferred me to the Alchemist.

---

37. *the mill*] a further allusion to the fact that the boys' father is a miller
(see 2.3.141–2n.).

37–8. *by imagination still*] on dreams of my expectations.

39–40. *looked . . . hands*] relied upon palmistry.

41. *nativity*] horoscope (based on the position of the stars at the moment
of birth).

46–8. *by these . . . Friday*] an allusion to the belief that each of the
planets governed a specific day of the week. Hence Rafe is a *Jovialist* in
that he was born on a Thursday (governed by Jupiter), and will be sexually
successful (*a brave Venerian*), and thus lucky on Fridays (governed by
Venus).

49. *strange . . . flesh day*] odd that a day on which fish (rather than meat)
is eaten (in Christian practice) should be a day for fleshly pursuits.

50. Venus orta mari] quoted from Ovid (*Heroides,* 15, 213). The passage,
which alludes to the myth that Venus sprang fully formed from the foam of
the sea, is translated by Rafe in the second half of the sentence.

51. *wine will have flesh*] intoxication leads to lechery.

52. caro . . . muliebre] flesh is feminine in gender. The line is quoted
from William Lily's Latin grammar, which formed the foundation of
the teaching of Latin in England at the period when the play was
composed.

53. *preferred me*] recommended me (with a view to employment).

Enter PETER.

Peter. [*To himself*] So I had a master, I would not care what
     became of me.   55
Rafe. [*Aside to Robin*] Robin, thou shalt see me fit him. [*More
     loudly*] So I had a servant, I care neither for his condi-
     tions, his qualities, nor his person.
Peter. What, Rafe? Well met! No doubt you had a warm service
     of my master the Alchemist?   60
Rafe. 'Twas warm indeed, for the fire had almost burnt out
     mine eyes, and yet my teeth still watered with hunger, so
     that my service was both too hot and too cold. I melted
     all my meat, and made only my slumber thoughts, and
     so had a full head and an empty belly. But where hast   65
     thou been since?
Peter. With a brother of thine, I think, for he hath such a coat,
     and two brothers (as he saith) seeking of fortunes.
Robin. 'Tis my brother Dick! I prithee, let's go to him.
Rafe. Sirrah, what was he doing that he came not with thee?   70
Peter. He hath gotten a master, now, that will teach him to
     make you both his younger brothers.
Rafe. Ay, thou passest for devising impossibilities! That's as
     true as thy master could make silver pots of tags of points.
Peter. Nay, he will teach him to cozen you both, and so get   75
     the mill to himself.

---

54. *So*] If only (also at line 57 below).

56. *fit him*] answer him in his own terms.

57–8. *care neither . . . person*] am indifferent to his style of life, his abilities,
or his appearance.

59–60. *warm service of*] (*a*) hard work being employed by; (*b*) hot work with.

63–4. *melted . . . meat*] melted down the money I had for food.

64. *made only . . . thoughts*] created nothing but dreams.

67. *hath such a coat*] is similarly dressed.

71–2. *He hath . . . brothers*] See Introduction p. 8 for the relationship
between the professions of the employers that the boys encounter in the
course of the play.

73. *thou passest*] you excel.

73–4. *as true . . . points*] See Peter's claims regarding the Alchemist's
powers at 2.3.44–5.

75–6. *he will . . . himself*] As the youngest brother (implied by lines 71–2
above and Rafe's response at lines 77–8 below), Dick could inherit their
father's mill at the period when the play was composed only if his two older
brothers predeceased him.

75. *cozen*] cheat.

Rafe. Nay, if he be both our cousins, I will be his great-
grandfather, and Robin shall be his uncle. But I pray thee,
bring us to him quickly, for I am great-bellied with
conceit till I see him.   80
Peter. Come, then, and go with me, and I will bring ye to him
straight.   *Exeunt.*

5.2.   [*Enter*] AUGUR [*and*] ERICTHINIS.

Augur. Bring forth the virgin, the fatal virgin, the fairest virgin,
if you mean to appease Neptune and preserve your country.
Ericthinis. Here she cometh, accompanied only with men,
because it is a sight unseemly (as all virgins say) to see
the misfortune of a maiden, and terrible to behold the   5
fierceness of Agar, that monster.

          Enter HEBE, *with others, to the sacrifice.*
          [HEBE *is bound to the tree.*]

Hebe. Miserable and accursed Hebe, that being neither fair nor
fortunate, thou shouldst be thought most happy and beautiful! Curse thy birth, thy life, thy death, being born to live
in danger, and, having lived, to die by deceit. Art thou the   10
sacrifice to appease Neptune and satisfy the custom, the
bloody custom, ordained for the safety of thy country? Ay,
Hebe, poor Hebe, men will have it so, whose forces

---

77. *both our cousins*] (*a*) kinsman to both of us (enabling the following
word-play on family relationships); (*b*) defrauder of us both (with a pun on
cozen at line 75 above).

77–8. *I will be . . . uncle*] Robin and I will prove his seniors in the art of
deception.

79–80. *great-bellied with conceit*] brimful of (literally 'heavily pregnant
with') anticipation.

82. *straight*] at once.

1. *the fatal virgin*] the maiden upon whom the destiny has fallen.

4. *unseemly*] improper.

6.1. others] The numerically indeterminate 'other' of the earliest edition
is emended to 'others' here, in that Ericthinis indicates at line 3 that Hebe
has more than one male attendant.

8. *happy*] fortunate.

10. *die by deceit*] Knowing that she is not the fairest virgin, Hebe is clearly
aware that some kind of deception is at work.

command our weak natures. Nay, the gods will have it so, whose powers dally with our purposes. The Egyptians   15 never cut their dates from the tree, because they are so fresh and green; it is thought wickedness to pull roses from the stalks in the garden of Palestine, for that they have so lively a red; and whoso cutteth the incense tree in Arabia before it fall committeth sacrilege. Shall it only be lawful   20 amongst us in the prime of youth and pride of beauty to destroy both youth and beauty; and what was honoured in fruits and flowers as a virtue, to violate in a virgin as a vice?

But, alas, destiny alloweth no dispute. Die, Hebe! Hebe die! Woeful Hebe, and only accursed Hebe! Farewell the   25 sweet delights of life, and welcome now the bitter pangs of death. Farewell you chaste virgins, whose thoughts are divine, whose faces fair, whose fortunes are agreeable to your affections. Enjoy, and long enjoy, the pleasure of your curled locks, the amiableness of your wished looks, the   30 sweetness of your tuned voices, the content of your inward thoughts, the pomp of your outward shows. Only Hebe biddeth farewell to all the joys that she conceived and you hope for, that she possessed and you shall. Farewell the pomp of princes' courts, whose roofs are embossed with   35 gold, and whose pavements are decked with fair ladies; where the days are spent in sweet delights, the nights in pleasant dreams; where chastity honoureth affections and commandeth, yieldeth to desire and conquereth.

---

15. *dally . . . purposes*] make sport of our plans.

15-20. *The Egyptians . . . sacrilege*] No precise source has been traced for any of these analogies, though some parallel formulations occur in Erasmus' *Parabolae*, to which Lyly is indebted in other works.

19. *whoso*] whoever.

20. *only*] uniquely.

28-9. *are agreeable . . . affections*] correspond to your desires.

30. *amiableness . . . looks*] loveliness of the looks you desire.

32. *pomp . . . shows*] splendour of your appearances.

Only Hebe] Hebe alone.

33. *conceived*] imagined.

34-9. *Farewell . . . conquereth*] Though superficially at odds with her lowly station in life, the widening circle of Hebe's lament accords with the pastoral tradition to which the drama belongs (see Introduction, pp. 10ff.) in which rustic figures are vehicles for reflections on matters

Farewell the sovereign of all virtues and goddess of all   40
virgins, Diana, whose perfections are impossible to be
numbered and therefore infinite, never to be matched,
and therefore immortal. Farewell sweet parents, yet, to be
mine, unfortunate parents! How blessed had you been in
barrenness; how happy had I been if I had not been! Fare-   45
well life, vain life, wretched life, whose sorrows are long,
whose end doubtful, whose miseries certain, whose hopes
innumerable, whose fears intolerable! Come, death, and
welcome, death, whom nature cannot resist because
necessity ruleth, nor defer because destiny hasteth. Come,   50
Agar, thou unsatiable monster of maidens' blood and
devourer of beauty's bowels. Glut thyself till thou surfeit,
and let my life end thine! Tear these tender joints with thy
greedy jaws, these yellow locks with thy black feet, this
fair face with thy foul teeth. Why abatest thou thy wonted   55
swiftness? I am fair, I am a virgin, I am ready! Come,
Agar, thou horrible monster; and farewell world, thou
viler monster.   [*There is no response.*]

Augur. The monster is not come, and therefore I see Neptune
is abused, whose rage will, I fear me, be both infinite and   60
intolerable. Take in this virgin, whose want of beauty hath
saved her own life, and [spoiled] all yours.

Ericthinis. We could not find any fairer.

Augur. Neptune will. Go, deliver her to her father.

[*Hebe is unbound.*]

---

pertinent to the aristocratic sphere (here, the courtly audience to which the
play is addressed).

38. *chastity honoureth affections*] desire is elevated by sexual restraint.

39. *yieldeth . . . conquereth*] gives place to desire and is triumphant (through
chaste marital love).

45. *if . . . been*] if I had not been born (with a pun on *been* in the same
line).

47. *doubtful*] uncertain.

55–6. *abatest . . . swiftness*] do you slacken your usual speed.

61. *want*] lack.

62. *spoiled*] destroyed. Omitted from the earliest edition, and initially supplied by Anne Lancashire, *spoiled* is preferred here before the 'destroyed' of
the previous Revels Plays edition for the characteristically Lylian alliteration
that it affords with the contrasting *saved* in the same line.

Hebe. Fortunate Hebe, how shalt thou express thy joys! Nay,   65
unhappy girl, that art not the fairest. Had it not been
better for thee to have died with fame than to live with
dishonour, to have preferred the safety of thy country and
rareness of thy beauty before sweetness of life and vanity
of the world? But, alas, destiny would not have it so,   70
destiny could not, because it asketh the beautifullest. I
would, Hebe, thou hadst been beautifullest.
Ericthinis. Come, Hebe, here is no time for us to reason. It
had been best for us thou hadst been most beautiful.

                                                  Exeunt.

5.3.   [*Enter*] PHILLIDA [*and*] GALATEA.

Phillida. We met the virgin that should have been offered to
Neptune. Belike the custom is pardoned, or she not
thought fairest.
Galatea. I cannot conjecture the cause, but I fear the event.
Phillida. Why should you fear? The god requireth no boy.   5
Galatea. I would he did; then should I have no fear.
Phillida. I am glad he doth not, though, because if he did, I
should have also cause to fear. [*She sees someone approach-
ing.*] But, soft, what man or god is this? Let us closely
withdraw ourselves into the thickets.   *Exeunt ambo.*   10

                Enter NEPTUNE *alone.*

Neptune. And do men begin to be equal with gods, seeking
by craft to overreach them that by power oversee them?

---

    71. *asketh*] requires.
    73. *reason*] discuss the matter.

    2. *Belike*] Perhaps, possibly.
    4. *conjecture*] surmise.
    event] outcome.
    6–8. *then should . . . to fear*] Being a girl, Galatea has no concern on her
own behalf should a boy be required for the sacrifice, whereas Phillida,
though also a girl, is afraid that Galatea, whom she assumes to be a boy,
might be chosen.
    9. *soft*] hush.
    closely] secretly.
    10. SD. ambo] both.
    12. *craft*] cunning (also at line 15 below).
    overreach] deceive.
    by power . . . them] govern them by power.

Do they dote so much on their daughters that they stick
not to dally with our deities? Well shall the inhabitants
see that destiny cannot be prevented by craft, nor my   15
anger appeased by submission. I will make havoc of
Diana's nymphs, my temple shall be dyed with maidens'
blood, and there shall be nothing more vile than to be a
virgin. To be young and fair shall be accounted shame
and punishment, insomuch as it shall be thought as dis-   20
honourable to be honest as fortunate to be deformed.

Enter DIANA *with her nymphs.*

Diana. Oh, Neptune, have you forgotten thyself, or wilt thou
clean forsake me? Hath Diana therefore brought danger
to her nymphs because they be chaste? Shall virtue suffer
both pain and shame, which always deserveth praise and   25
honour?

Enter VENUS.

Venus. Praise and honour, Nepune? Nothing less, except it be
commendable to be coy and honourable to be peevish.
Sweet Neptune, if Venus can do anything, let her try it in
this one thing, that Diana may find as small comfort at   30
thy hands as love hath found courtesy at hers. This is she
[*Pointing to Diana*] that hateth sweet delights, envieth
loving desires, masketh wanton eyes, stoppeth amorous
ears, bridleth youthful mouths, and under a name, or a
word, 'constancy', entertaineth all kind of cruelty. She   35
hath taken my son, Cupid, Cupid my lovely son, using
him like a prentice, whipping him like a slave, scorning

13–14. *stick . . . dally*] do not scruple to toy.
15. *prevented*] forestalled.
21. *honest*] chaste.
28. *coy*] disdainful.
peevish] perverse.
29. *can do anything*] has any influence with you.
32. *envieth*] is malicious towards.
33. *masketh*] covers.
34. *bridleth*] curbs.
35. *entertaineth*] sanctions, promotes.
37. *prentice*] apprentice.

him like a beast. Therefore, Neptune, I entreat thee, by
no other god than the god of love, that thou evil entreat
this goddess of hate.   40

Neptune. I muse not a little to see you two in this place, at
this time, and about this matter. But what say you, Diana?
Have you Cupid captive?

Diana. I say that there is nothing more vain than to dispute
with Venus, whose untamed affections have bred more   45
brawls in heaven than is fit to repeat in earth, or possible
to recount in number. I have Cupid, and will keep him,
not to dandle in my lap, whom I abhor in my heart, but
to laugh him to scorn, that hath made in my virgins'
hearts such deep scars.   50

Venus. Scars, Diana, call you them that I know to be bleeding
wounds? Alas, weak deity, it stretcheth not so far both to
abate the sharpness of his arrows and to heal the hurts.
No, love's wounds, when they seem green, rankle, and,
having a smooth skin without, fester to the death within.   55
Therefore, Neptune, if ever Venus stood thee in stead,
furthered thy fancies, or shall at all times be at thy
command, let either Diana bring her virgins to a mas-
sacre, or release Cupid of his martyrdom.

Diana. It is known, Venus, that your tongue is as unruly as   60
your thoughts, and your thoughts as unstayed as your
eyes. Diana cannot chatter; Venus cannot choose.

Venus. It is an honour for Diana to have Venus mean ill, when
she so speaketh well. But you shall see I come not to trifle.
Therefore, once again, Neptune, if that be not buried   65

---

39. *evil entreat*] behave with harshness towards.
41. *muse not a little*] am considerably perplexed.
48. *dandle*] fondle (literally 'bounce up and down').
52. *it stretcheth . . . far*] your power does not extend far enough.
53. *abate*] blunt.
54. *green, rankle*] fresh, fester.
55. *without*] on the outside.
56. *stood thee in stead*] was of service to you.
57. *furthered thy fancies*] promoted your desires.
61. *unstayed*] ungoverned.
62. *choose*] help herself (chattering).
63–4. *It is . . . well*] I am flattered that Diana should find my words offen-
sive when she is capable of such speeches as these.

which can never die – fancy – or that quenched which
must ever burn – affection – show thyself the same
Neptune that I knew thee to be when thou wast a shepherd, and let not Venus' words be vain in thine ears, since
thine were imprinted in my heart.   70

Neptune. It were unfit that goddesses should strive, and it
were unreasonable that I should not yield, and therefore,
to please both, attend. Diana I must honour, her virtue
deserveth no less; but Venus I must love, I must confess
so much. [*He turns to Diana.*] Diana, restore Cupid to   75
Venus, and I will for ever release the sacrifice of virgins.
If, therefore, you love your nymphs as she doth her son,
or prefer not a private grudge before a common grief,
answer what you will do.

Diana. I account not the choice hard, for had I twenty Cupids   80
I would deliver them all to save one virgin, knowing love
to be a thing of all the vainest, virginity to be a virtue of
all the noblest. I yield. Larissa, bring out Cupid. [*Exit
LARISSA.*] And now shall it be said that Cupid saved
those he thought to spoil.   85

Venus. I agree to this willingly, for I will be wary how my son
wander again. But Diana cannot forbid him to wound.

Diana. Yes, chastity is not within the level of his bow.

Venus. But beauty is a fair mark to hit.

---

66. *fancy*] amorous inclination.

67. *affection*] desire.

68–9. *when . . . shepherd*] Neptune assumed a number of disguises in order
to fulfil his sexual desires, but no precise source has been found for this
allusion. Given the fact that Venus herself was among those that he pursued,
however, it may be that the term 'shepherd' here carries its pastoral connotations of 'lover' or 'suitor'.

69. *vain*] without effect, unavailing.

70. *thine*] your words.

73. *attend*] listen.

78. *prefer not . . . grief*] do not rate a private quarrel above a universal
affliction.

82. *vainest*] most futile.

84–5. *saved . . . spoil*] rescued the virgins he intended to harm (in that his
restoration to Venus admits the remission of the virgin sacrifice).

88. *level*] range.

89. *fair mark*] (*a*) agreeable object; (*b*) legitimate target.

Neptune. Well, I am glad you are agreed, and say that Neptune   90
  hath dealt well with beauty and chastity.

              Enter [LARISSA *with*] CUPID.

Diana. [*To Venus*] Here, take your son.
Venus. Sir boy, where have you been? Always taken, first by
  Sappho, now by Diana. How happeneth it, you unhappy elf?
Cupid. Coming through Diana's woods, and seeing so many   95
  fair faces with fond hearts, I thought for my sport to make
  them smart, and so was taken by Diana.
Venus. I am glad I have you.
Diana. And I am glad I am rid of him.
Venus. Alas, poor boy! Thy wings clipped? Thy brands   100
  quenched? Thy bow burnt, and thy arrows broke?
Cupid. Ay, but it skilleth not. I bear now mine arrows in mine
  eyes, my wings on my thoughts, my brands in mine ears,
  my bow in my mouth; so as I can wound with looking,
  fly with thinking, burn with hearing, shoot with   105
  speaking.
Venus. Well, you shall up to heaven with me, for on earth thou
  wilt lose me.

              Enter TITYRUS [*and*] MELIBEUS.

Neptune. But soft, what be these?
Tityrus. Those that have offended thee to save their   110
  daughters.
Neptune. Why, had you a fair daughter?

---

90. *agreed*] in accord.
93–4. *first by Sappho*] an allusion to Lyly's previous play, *Sappho and Phao*,
in which Cupid transfers his loyalty from his mother to Sappho. The reference implies that the audience at the original performance would have been
conscious of the earlier play.
94. *happeneth it*] does it come about.
unhappy elf] unfortunate little imp.
96–7. *my sport . . . smart*] my pleasure to cause them pain.
100–1. *Thy wings . . . broke*] See Diana's threats at 3.4.85–7.
100. *brands*] firebrands, torches (also at line 103 below).
102. *skilleth not*] does not matter.
104. *as*] that.
107. *up*] come up.
109. *soft*] wait a moment.

Tityrus. Ay, and Melibeus a fair daughter.

Neptune. Where be they?

Melibeus. In yonder woods; and methinks I see them coming.   115

Neptune. Well, your deserts have not gotten pardon, but these
     goddesses' jars.

> [*Enter*] GALATEA *and* PHILLIDA.

Melibeus. This is my daughter, my sweet Phillida.

Tityrus. And this is my fair Galatea.

Galatea. Unfortunate Galatea, if this be Phillida!   120

Phillida. Accursed Phillida, if that be Galatea!

Galatea. And wast thou, all this while, enamoured of Phillida,
     that sweet Phillida?

Phillida. And couldst thou dote upon the face of a maiden,
     thyself being one, on the face of fair Galatea?   125

Neptune. Do you both, being maidens, love one another?

Galatea. I had thought the habit agreeable with the sex, and
     so burned in the fire of my own fancies.

Phillida. I had thought that in the attire of a boy there could
     not have lodged the body of a virgin, and so was inflamed   130
     with a sweet desire which now I find a sour deceit.

Diana. Now, things falling out as they do, you must leave
     these fond, fond affections. Nature will have it so; neces-
     sity must.

Galatea. I will never love any but Phillida; her love is engraven   135
     in my heart with her eyes.

Phillida. Nor I any but Galatea; whose faith is imprinted in
     my thoughts by her words.

Neptune. An idle choice, strange and foolish, for one virgin to
     dote on another, and to imagine a constant faith where   140
     there can be no cause of affection. – How like you this,
     Venus?

---

116. *deserts . . . pardon*] behaviour hasn't procured you this act of
clemency.

117. *jars*] quarrels.

122. *enamoured of*] in love with.

127. *habit . . . sex*] garments were in accordance with the gender.

128. *fancies*] desires.

133. *fond, fond*] foolish, doting.

141. *cause of affection*] instigation to sexual desire.

Venus. I like well, and allow it. They shall both be possessed
of their wishes, for never shall it be said that Nature or
Fortune shall overthrow Love and Faith. [*To Galatea and*   145
Phillida] Is your loves unspotted, begun with truth, con-
tinued with constancy, and not to be altered till death?
Galatea. Die, Galatea, if thy love be not so!
Phillida. Accursed be thou, Phillida, if thy love be not so!
Diana. Suppose all this, Venus, what then?   150
Venus. Then shall it be seen that I can turn one of them to be
a man, and that I will.
Diana. Is it possible?
Venus. What is to love, or the mistress of love, unpossible? Was
it not Venus that did the like to Iphis and Ianthes? [*To*   155
Galatea and Phillida] How say ye, are ye agreed, one to
be a boy presently?
Phillida. I am content, so I may embrace Galatea.
Galatea. I wish it, so I may enjoy Phillida.
Melibeus. Soft, daughter, you must know whether I will have   160
you a son.
Tityrus. Take me with you, Galatea. I will keep you as I begat
you, a daughter.
Melibeus. Tityrus, let yours be a boy, and if you will; mine shall
not.   165
Tityrus. Nay, mine shall not; for by that means my young son
shall lose his inheritance.

---

143. *allow*] approve.
150. *Suppose all this*] Even supposing this to be the case.
155. *Iphis and Ianthes*] Having been brought up as a boy to circumvent
an edict passed by her father, Iphis was betrothed to another maiden, Ianthe.
Their union was facilitated by the goddess Isis (equated in the late Greek
period with Aphrodite, i.e. Roman Venus) through the transformation of
Iphis into a youth.
157. *presently*] immediately.
159. *enjoy*] consummate my love for.
160. *Soft*] Just a moment.
162. *Take me with you*] Don't forget me.
164. *and if you will*] if you like.
166–7. *for by . . . inheritance*] Whereas, being a girl, Galatea would not
inherit from her father should he have a son of any age, as the older child
she would take precedence over her brother once transformed into a youth.

Melibeus. Why then, get him to be made a maiden, and then
    there is nothing lost.
Tityrus. If there be such changing, I would Venus could make   170
    my wife a man.
Melibeus. Why?
Tityrus. Because she loves always to play with men.
Venus. Well, you are both fond. Therefore agree to this chang-
    ing, or suffer your daughters to endure hard chance.   175
Melibeus. How say you, Tityrus, shall we refer it to Venus?
Tityrus. I am content, because she is a goddess.
Venus. Neptune, you will not mislike it?
Neptune. Not I.
Venus. Nor you, Diana?   180
Diana. Not I.
Venus. Cupid shall not.
Cupid. I will not.
Venus. Then let us depart. Neither of them shall know whose
    lot it shall be till they come to the church door. One shall   185
    be. Doth it suffice?
Phillida. And satisfy us both, doth it not, Galatea?
Galatea. Yes, Phillida.

              Enter RAFE, ROBIN, *and* DICK.

Rafe. Come, Robin, I am glad I have met with thee, for now
    we will make our father laugh at these tales.   190

168–9. *get him . . . lost*] If the younger of the two children were transformed into a girl, he would no longer have any claim on the family estate,
and the property would pass, as before, to a son (i.e. the metamorphosed
Galatea).

    173. *play*] dally (with sexual connotations).

    174. *fond*] foolish.

    175. *suffer*] permit.

    hard chance] a harsh fate.

    176. *refer it to Venus*] leave the matter to Venus to decide.

    185. *lot*] fate.

    church door] Marriages were celebrated at this period at the church door,
rather than within the main body of the church.

    186. *Doth it suffice*] Is that enough (for you).

Diana. What are these that so malapertly thrust themselves
   into our companies?

Robin. Forsooth, madam, we are fortune tellers.

Venus. Fortune-tellers? Tell me my fortune.

Rafe. We do not mean fortune-tellers; we mean fortune tellers.   195
   We can tell what fortune we have had these twelve months
   in the woods.

Diana. Let them alone; they be but peevish.

Venus. Yet they will be as good as minstrels at the marriage,
   to make us all merry.   200

Dick. Ay, ladies, we bear a good consort.

Venus. Can you sing?

Rafe. Basely.

Venus. And you?

Dick. Meanly.   205

Venus. And what can you do?

Robin. If they double it, I will treble it.

Venus. Then shall ye go with us, and sing Hymen before the
   marriage. Are you content?

Rafe. Content? Never better content, for there we shall be   210
   sure to fill our bellies with capons, rumps, or some such
   dainty dishes.

Venus. Then follow us.   *Exeunt [all but* GALATEA].

---

191. *malapertly*] impudently.

193, 194. *fortune tellers / Fortune-tellers*] people able to recount their adventures (the meaning Robin intends) / people able to foretell the future (the
sense in which Venus understands him). The distinction between the two
terms is clarified by Rafe in the following lines.

198. *Let them . . . peevish*] Ignore them, they are just perverse.

201. *bear . . . consort*] carry a good harmony.

203–7.] The boys' response to Venus' question at line 202 involves a series
of puns on the parts taken by the singers of a three-part song or round. Rafe
claims that he can sing the bass part, while implying he sings badly; Dick
indicates that he can sing the tenor part, while suggesting that he has an
average voice; and Robin asserts that he can sing the treble part, while declar-
ing (*a*) that he can turn a two-part song into one for three voices; (*b*) that
whatever his brothers can do he can do three times as well.

208. *sing Hymen*] perform a marriage song.

Hymen] the Greek god of marriage (cf. the role played by the figure in
the closing scene of *As You Like It*).

209. *content*] satisfied, happy with this.

210. *Content / content*] Pleased / stuffing.

211. *capons*] gelded cocks fattened for the table.

rumps] portions of meat taken from an animal's hind parts.

The Epilogue

[GALATEA *comes forward.*]

Galatea. Go all, 'tis I only that conclude all. You ladies may
see that Venus can make constancy fickleness, courage
cowardice, modesty lightness, working things impossible
in your sex, and tempering hardest hearts like softest
wool. Yield, ladies, yield to love, ladies, which lurketh   5
under your eyelids whilst you sleep, and playeth with your
heartstrings whilst you wake; whose sweetness never
breedeth satiety, labour weariness, nor grief bitterness.
Cupid was begotten in a mist, nursed in clouds, and
sucking only upon conceits. Confess him a conqueror,   10
whom ye ought to regard, sith it is unpossible to resist;
for this is infallible, that love conquereth all things but
itself, and ladies all hearts but their own.   [*Exit.*]

FINIS

---

1. *only*] alone.

3. *lightness*] wantonness.

4. *tempering*] softening.

8. *labour . . . bitterness*] whose demands never induce tiredness and whose
pangs never promote bitterness (elliptical formulation).

10. *sucking . . . conceits*] fed only on thoughts.

11. *regard*] respect, venerate.

12. *infallible*] incontrovertible.

13. *ladies all hearts*] ladies conquer all hearts (elliptical formulation).

13.1. *FINIS*] The end.

EU authorised representative for GPSR:
Easy Access System Europe, Mustamäe tee 50,
10621 Tallinn, Estonia
gpsr.requests@easproject.com

www.ingramcontent.com/pod-product-compliance
Lightning Source LLC
Chambersburg PA
CBHW052113090426
42741CB00009B/1791